Gail Vines read biology and philosophy at Vassar, and did field research in animal behaviour at Aberdeen and Bristol. She joined *New Scientist* as life sciences editor, was features editor from 1986 to 1992, and is now its life sciences consultant. She has twice won the Glaxo/Association of British Science Writers Award for science journalism and was Consumer Journalist of the Year at the Periodical Press Association Awards in 1990. Her previous, co-authored, books are *The Evolution of Life* (1986), and *Tomorrow's Child* (Virago, 1990). Now a freelance science journalist specialising in biology and medicine, she lives in Cambridge.

D1329977

GAIL VINES

RAGING HORMONES

DO THEY RULE OUR LIVES?

UNIVERSITY OF CALIFORNIA PRESS   BERKELEY   LOS ANGELES

University of California Press
Berkeley and Los Angeles, California

Copyright © Gail Vines 1993

First Edition published by Virago Press, London, 1993

First University of California Press Edition, 1994

Library of Congress Cataloging-in-Publication Data

Vines, Gail.
Raging hormones : Do they rule our lives? / Gail Vines.
p.   cm.
Includes bibliographical references and index.
ISBN 0-520-08776-3 (alk. paper).—
ISBN 0-520-08777-1 (alk. paper : pbk.)
1. Hormones.   2. Psychoneuroendocrinology.   3. Sex
differences.   4. Endocrinology—History.   I. Title.
QP571.V56   1994
612.4—dc20   93-44921
                                                         CIP

Printed in the United States of America
9   8   7   6   5   4   3   2   1

CONTENTS

PREFACE

The 1990s seem set to witness a resurgence in 'biological' explanations of human capabilities and frailties. The human genome project, hailed as the search for the ultimate genetic 'blueprint' of humanity, is gathering momentum. Meanwhile, a leading American research agency has declared this 'the decade of the brain'. At the same time, techniques for detecting hormones in blood and saliva continue to improve, making it likely that these chemical mediators between genes and brain will retain much of their appeal as potent 'causes' of human behaviour.

Many commentators see nothing amiss in this fervour for explanations framed on the inner workings of the body, with hormones playing a leading role. Yet all too often, the insights that come from both cross-cultural and historical perspectives are overlooked, and the authority of biomedical science to define both the 'problem' and its solution remains largely unchallenged.

Raging Hormones sets out to show the extent to which medical and scientific discourse on hormones is not simply about a class of biochemicals and their effects. Time and again, hormones also seem to be standing in for something else. Throughout the twentieth century, these molecules have been loaded with powerful symbolic meanings that reflect a remarkable array of shifting, and often conflicting, social and cultural preoccupations. *Raging Hormones* attempts to show just a few of the ways in which scientific research and medical practice are embedded in contemporary culture.

Many people have supported this project. I would especially like to thank Frances Price for her invaluable comments and criticism, but most of all for her friendship and encouragement throughout the preparation of this book. I am also grateful to Alice Henry, Ruth Wallsgrove and Alyish Wood, who generously agreed to read a draft at very short notice. Their comments greatly improved the final product. I also thank Germaine Greer and Susie Orbach, who kindly read and commented on the manuscript for Virago. My thanks also go to my friends and colleagues at *New Scientist* who, over many years, have shown that science journalism can be both challenging and a good read. I am indebted to Beth Humphries and Gillian Beaumont for their skillful copyediting, and Melanie Silgardo at Virago Press for her enthusiasm for the project, and her patience. I would finally like to thank Naomi Schneider and the readers of the University of California Press for suggesting many improvements for the American edition.

INTRODUCTION

In the early decades of the twentieth century, hormones excited scientists as much as genes do today. They were regarded as 'signal' molecules, the body's premier chemical messengers. It seemed so persuasive, the idea that the study of the chemical secretions of a dozen or so glands could reveal how we are, and why we behave in the way we do.

Hormones have now become part of our day-to-day language, a way of accounting for our own and other people's behaviour. The butt of jokes, they feature seriously in law. A bodybuilder who killed his children by setting fire to his home can claim that he was driven by 'steroid rages'.[1] The very word 'hormone' implies reckless action. Scientists coined the term in 1905, from a Greek verb meaning 'to stir up, urge on', and the noun for 'impulse'. Lawyers can plead for clemency for female clients on grounds of premenstrual hormone imbalance.[2] Meanwhile, menopausal women are encouraged to seek 'hormone replacement therapy'.

The belief that hormones have the power to control what we feel and how we behave runs deep in scientific and popular culture alike. But the chemical underpinnings of human

1

behaviour continue to elude the scientists. The data are contradictory, the evidence is contested, the picture grows ever more complex. Yet the fundamental research programme continues, its conceptual framework apparently unassailable.

Something strange is happening here. Both the controversy surrounding hormones and behaviour, and the persistence with which a link is sought, suggest the impact of powerful cultural imperatives. The fact that hormones are most often seen as 'something women have' is, as we shall see, most revealing of all.

The Rage for Hormones

Hormones have become inexorably linked with particular 'effects'. Scientists took out glands and then put them back, or injected pulverised extracts and watched what happened. They marked the waxing and waning of a cockerel's comb, and charted the swelling and shrinking of a rat's testicles. Such physical changes became markers of a hormone's presence, and enabled researchers to isolate hormones from messy glandular extracts. Scientists who specialised in the study of hormones – endocrinologists – came to believe that judicious injections of purified glandular extracts would hold the key to everything from bird migration to human aggression. An animal's behaviour came to be seen as just another hormonal effect.

In laboratory rats, researchers expected to find one hormone for male libido, another for female. When, in 1935, Oscar Riddle and his colleagues isolated the hormone prolactin in nesting ring doves, their discovery was heralded as the key to 'maternal instinct'.[3] The lack of the right hormonal complement was later linked to both postnatal depression and a failure to 'bond' with the child, leading to 'bad' mothering.

Yet the endocrinologists' desire to answer the question 'which hormone brings about what behaviour?' was continually frustrated.[4] The discrepancies became increasingly glaring as researchers moved from fish, reptiles and birds to mammals. Behavioural scientists had to resign themselves to the fact that hormones were not living up to expectations.

But the quest continues. Today, the focus of research is on

2

the action of hormones on the brain, 'the organ of behaviour'. New specialisms have sprung up, linking hormones, brain and behaviour. Yet while many specialists in these fields are convinced that they will ultimately be able to explain human behaviour, they emphasise the enormity of the project and the complexity of the 'causal nexus'.

In their preface to a leading textbook published in 1990, *Hormones: From Molecules to Disease*, Etienne-Emile Baulieu and Paul Kelly acknowledge the multifarious ways in which the social and physical environment can alter a person's hormones: 'Hormones respond to changes in brain activity, and to physiological, environmental and social influences, so endocrinology can be truly called a *humanistic* science.'[5] The authors might audaciously be proposing that the social sciences should be seen as branches of endocrinology – that life can be reduced to the waxing and waning of hormones. Yet they are quick to qualify any claim to hold the key to human understanding: 'But since unexpected levels of complexity of hormonal systems are continually being unearthed, it seems apparent that – in spite of our optimism – any notion of "state-of-the-art" is ephemeral.'

Monkey Business

An international meeting of primatologists, held in Brazil in July 1988, reflected the tensions evident in contemporary hormonal research.[6] A symposium was devoted to the new field of 'socioendocrinology', defined as the study of the links between the social environment, hormones and behaviour. The organisers of the symposium, Fred Berkovitch and Toni Ziegler of the University of Wisconsin, see hormones as providing the body 'with a method to respond to the external environment'. Hormones become a tool of the organism, not its taskmaster, and allow 'the body to be flexible under changing social environments'. They emphasise 'interactions' and speak of flexibility and change.

Another American primatologist at the conference, Carol Worthman, spelt out the apparently radical agenda of the new discipline. Endocrinology erred in its early days 'for the sake of expediency'. It was far easier to ignore an animal's social context and think of hormones as having a fixed effect. This empirical tradition fostered a view of hormones as causes of behaviour, Worthman argued, rather than as participants in a web of regulation.

The study of monkeys and apes, humanity's closest relatives, has threatened the classical view. The complexity of the social worlds they inhabit militates against simple chemical triggers for particular actions.[7] Even monkeys are not slaves to their hormones, argues Barry Keverne, director of the sub-department of animal behaviour at the University of Cambridge. The sexual behaviour of the monkeys he studies is not tied to the neuroendocrine events that determine ovulation or sperm production. Indeed, most sexual encounters take place outside the female's fertile period, or during pregnancy. The monkeys' complex social interactions are the key to understanding sex and reproduction; in our primate relatives, behaviour has become 'emancipated' from sex hormones, Keverne argues. And if monkeys and apes are not controlled by their hormones, primatologists conclude, there seems little reason to suppose that human beings are.

One recent study suggests that hormones do not 'cause' sexual behaviour even in birds. Through a series of rather grisly experiments involving surgically deafening and silencing female doves, Mei-Fang Cheng of Rutgers University in New Jersey has demonstrated that the females normally 'talk' to their ovaries. It is the female's own cooing, not the courtship of the male, that stimulates the hormonal changes needed to trigger the release of a mature egg. The presence of the male is important only in that he stimulates the female to make this noise. Cheng says hers is the first example of an animal making sounds that alter its own internal state.[8]

Identity Crisis

Hormones themselves are becoming harder to defend as classical chemical messengers – as a special class of chemicals with independent effects. To classify as a hormone in the traditional sense, a molecule must travel through the bloodstream to some distant target cells. These target cells define themselves by their possession of the appropriate receptor – a distinctive molecular hook or docking site that can recognise and physically latch on to a particular hormone. The fusion of hormone and receptor in turn sets off a chemical chain reaction, a cascade of biochemical events, which may activate certain genes and eventually lead to changes in what particular cells do. For instance, hair sprouts out of dormant follicles, breast cells multiply, fat deposits expand, all in response to oestrogens surging from a girl's ovaries at puberty.

So a hormone's effects can radically alter, depending on which cells are displaying how many of the appropriate receptors. For instance, it does not matter how much hormone someone has in their blood if receptors are thin on the ground, and all sorts of factors can influence receptor status. Moreover, hormones can become inactivated if they attach to binding proteins in the blood. These chemicals are also destroyed at different rates in different circumstances. Hormones circulating in the blood are heir to a variety of metabolic onslaughts, especially from the liver, fat tissue and kidneys; most hormone molecules are destroyed even before they encounter any receptor-laden cells. The target site itself often chemically alters the hormone, and so enhances or lessens its effects. Finally, complex feedback loops involving many different chemical interactions influence how much hormone the glandular cells continue to produce.

Hormones that circulate in the bloodstream can also be released locally, to influence the cells that produce them (an autocrine effect) or to act on neighbouring cells, a phenomenon known as a paracrine effect (from the Greek *para*, 'to the side'). One hormone, somatostatin, was originally discovered in the hypothalamus in the brain, but it also acts as a local hormone in the pancreas. Insulin and steroids, once thought to be made only by the pancreas and sex organs respectively, are also produced in the brain. Many other messenger chemicals, such as various growth factors, are manufactured by cells that are not organised into glands, yet they may act much as the traditional hormones do.

5

Classically, hormones were thought of as robust chemical signals that surged through the bloodstream towards their target tissues. Nerves spoke a completely different language, and a private one at that. Their chemical messengers merely linked one nerve cell to another, passing on an electrical signal like so much telegraph wire. Now this distinction is becoming increasingly blurred. For instance, molecules which everyone thought were classic hormones have since turned up in nerve cells in the brain. Chemical communication by nerve and hormone represents a continuum, not rigidly alternative systems. And evidence is growing that the endocrine system, the immune system and nervous system all interact at many levels. Complex neural and feedback networks integrate a vast array of information garnered from inside and outside the body. Recent research on birds, for instance, suggests that their brain cells possess the enzymes necessary to either activate or inactivate sex hormones, and that their social environment influences which enzymes are active.[9]

So some researchers have shifted away from the 'hormone-behaviour' determinism so popular in the 1960s and 1970s. Today, a recent textbook concludes, a wise endocrinologist avoids dogmatic predictions about precisely what any one hormone will do, for what hormones do depends on the circumstances.[10] The most you can safely say, Baulieu and Kelly conclude, is that hormones 'are modulators of the potential of each specific cell'. A cell's potential, they say, is defined by what kind of cell it is, but also 'circumstantially, by age, metabolism, activity, etc.'. Elsewhere, Baulieu reminds fellow scientists that hormones do not simply determine behaviour: 'one should not forget', he says, 'that the state of neural activity is also related to action, emotion and thinking'. Yet as one scientist in the field wrote recently:

> the trend in behavioural neuroendocrinology is to focus on a single sex, a single behaviour, or a single hormone. This is evident in studies in which the investigator may spend years determining the reproductive cycle in the male (or female) while ignoring the potential contribution of the partner.[11]

6

Why this tension in current scientific practice? Why do some scientists make bold claims about the links between hormones and behaviour, while others are more cautious? Why are some reluctant, and others eager, to extrapolate from experiments on laboratory animals to humans? It is tempting to conclude that one sort of science is 'good', the other 'bad', but it is difficult to substantiate any such claim.[12] What we need to understand are the ways in which larger social and cultural concerns impinge on what can appear to be simply scientific, technical debates about the relationship between human experience and inner chemistry.

Whose Hormones?

One of the central themes that emerges from a look at the science of hormones is the distinctly different ways in which hormonal accounts have been applied to women and men. Hormones are frequently proffered as explanations of women's everyday experience – so much so that a tendency to 'hormonal imbalance' has become a defining characteristic of women today. The situation is subtly different for men. 'Male' hormones are typically regarded as the source of male violence and sexual aggressiveness, yet this is rarely viewed as a problem. Male hormones are treated as pathological only among men regarded as 'deviant' – homosexuals, criminals and mental patients, for instance – and even then there is a marked reluctance to manipulate a man's hormonal makeup. The typical contemporary male, supposedly invigorated by testosterone, is culturally accommodated; the normal woman, by contrast, may be encouraged to seek medical assistance to control her raging hormones. Women are expected to manage and to take responsibility for their own hormonal states, but they are also expected to tolerate, and to manage the best they can, the hormonally induced behaviour of men.

Men have long regarded themselves as potentially under threat from the hormonally deranged woman. Now the hormones themselves seem to be at large in the environment, endangering the very foundation of masculinity. There have long been rumours that the breakdown products of oral contraceptives in women's urine somehow find their way back into the drinking water, to pose a threat to male virility. Recently, oestrogens in the environment have again made the headlines, after two scientists reported that various synthetic chemicals, including some pesticides and detergents, can mimic oestrogens.[13] Such pollutants, the researchers suggested, might have contributed to the demonstrable rise in the rate of testicular cancer, and to the apparent fall in sperm counts, over the past fifty years. The scientists hypothesise that the damage is done by the exposure of vulnerable male fetuses to an overdose of oestrogen in their mothers' womb.

There is much debate about whether the levels of synthetic oestrogens in the environment are great enough to have any significant effect on a fetus's exposure levels: pregnant women produce high levels of the hormone in any case. But on the face of it, this potentially alarming story seems free of gender bias – it is taken for granted that men will be at risk from contamination by the essence of woman, the 'female' sex hormone. 'Men who complain they are at the mercy of female hormones may be closer to the truth than they realise,' writes Jenny Hope, medical correspondent of the *Daily Mail*.[14] 'For the latest scientific thinking argues that while we are all living in a world that is a "virtual sea of oestrogens",' Hope claims, 'it is men that are suffering. The very concept of manhood appears to be under threat.' According to Hope, oestrogens are 'subtly feminising' men in the womb and during childhood.

Yet oestrogens are naturally present in both men and women, where the hormones perform a variety of functions related to cell growth and development. At the same time, women too may be at risk from excess oestrogen from the environment – as suggested by the growing evidence that oestrogens in contraceptive pills and hormone replacement therapy increase the risk that women will develop breast cancer or cancers of the reproductive tract. The newspaper reports all used the vocabulary of 'a sea of oestrogen' and the threat to masculinity; no reporter looked beyond the sex stereotype to explore what might really be going on.

The 'Discovery' of Sex

The origins of this urge to see women as the hormonal sex stretch back several centuries. The contemporary concern to discover biological differences between the sexes – and thus to ground socially constructed gender roles in something seemingly fixed, immutable, given – is by no means unique to our time. The current drive to compare and contrast bits of male and female physiology is only the latest development in a scientific tradition that dates from the Enlightenment. The fascination with difference seems to have begun then. Before the eighteenth century, medical opinion saw women as intrinsically like men: they were inferior, certainly, but they were regarded as variations on a single theme. There was only one sex, really. Women differed in their sexual anatomy, but only as an obverse of men: the vagina was an interior penis, the womb was a scrotum, the ovaries were testicles. In this pre-Enlightenment view, as the historian Thomas Laqueur recounts in his book *Making Sex*, the body represented, but did not determine, social gender.[15]

With the Enlightenment a new philosophy came to predominate – the notion that there are two sexes, with woman the opposite of man, with inexorably different organs, functions and feelings. The point here is not that pre-Enlightenment folk got their anatomy wrong – every generation finds fault with its ancestors' received wisdom. The crucial point is that since the Enlightenment the body has been seen as determining gender differences.

The history of sexual science over the past three centuries shows just how powerful is the cultural imperative to scour the body for signs of difference, which can then be used to justify gender-based social distinctions. Drawing on Victorian debates, Cynthia Eagle Russet finds examples to substantiate her claim that science and medicine of the day helped to maintain a social order structured around gender, class and race.[16] She argues that the spur for much research lay in the perceived threat of newly assertive women seeking to enrol in universities or enter the professions. Woman's sexual difference, and concomitant unsuitability for a life outside the domestic sphere, was variously attributed to the size of her skull, an affinity with lower organisms, arrested development, maternal destiny and criminal tendencies.

Londa Schiebinger argues that our current understanding of biological difference between men and women developed from Victorian notions of 'complementarity' – the belief that there are 'natural' and clear-cut mental and physical differences between the sexes which translate directly into separate roles within society.[17] Anatomical differences were used to bolster the argument that 'moral and intellectual qualities were innate and enduring as the bones of the body'. She, too, points to the cultural 'discovery' of gender during the Enlightenment. Early anatomical illustrations of male and female skeletons were indifferent to dissimilarities between the sexes, and often failed to give the sex of an illustrated figure. But by the mid eighteenth century, the artists often deliberately exaggerated the differences, inflating the size of the female's pelvis and shrinking her head and ribcage to correspond to emerging ideas of masculine and feminine.

Theories come and go as new findings conflict with the received view, but gender remains central to science and medicine. Indeed, as Ludmilla Jordanova has cogently argued, gender, as one of the strongest determinants of personal identity and social relations, profoundly influences scientific conceptions of 'natural knowledge' – the construction of ideas about what is there to be studied, categorised, discovered.[18] In a striking way, recent debates about phenomena as diverse as homosexuality, premenstrual syndrome and sex therapy variously echo these historical themes.

Body Politics

Hormonal accounts play another, related, role in contemporary culture. Hormones have an enduring appeal for late-twentieth-century Euro-Americans, because they epitomise the central concern with 'control'. Current conceptualisations of aggression, stress and eating disorders – all linked to hormones in various ways – reveal a shared concern with some inner process in danger of exploding out of control. Individuals are expected to 'manage' appropriately these bodily impulses and desires, and seek medical help when there is a problem with 'self-control'.

Contemporary preoccupation with internal body management reflects the contradictory pressures and tensions of modern social and economic life. Cultural anxieties about the regulation of desire in consumption-driven capitalist societies become displaced on to the body. As the anthropologist Mary Douglas has argued, the body becomes a system of 'natural symbols' that reproduce social categories and concerns.[19] Thus the images of the physical body – the microcosm – may symbolically reproduce the central vulnerabilities and anxieties of the macrocosm – the 'social body'. In patriarchal systems, men's fears are readily transposed on to women, already seen as the 'other', against which they organise their identities. Women then become defined as inherently unstable, in danger of running out of containment, in contrast with rational, self-determining man.

What can be said about the role of hormones in our lives? This book explores the question by drawing from psychology, anthropology, sociology and the history of medicine, as well as from biology and medical sciences. The focus is on what scientists call 'behaviour' – on the claims made about the role of hormones in determining what we do, and how we think and feel. The aim is to examine the enduring appeal of images of humanity driven by internal chemicals. The pronouncements of modern science are inevitably framed by history, and by contemporary social concerns such as who is a suitable case for treatment.

A deeper understanding of the origins of current ideas about how hormones work may help us to regain a sense of connection with our bodies and our environment in the broadest sense – to appreciate the links between the way we are and the way we live, to look at our lives in context. Such empowerment will come only with the knowledge that in reality, collectively and individually, we are continually creating ourselves.

HORMONES OF DESIRE

THE WELLSPRINGS
OF LIBIDO?

I f endocrinologists had a coat of arms, the cockerel rampant would have pride of place. For when they come to write text-books, these researchers routinely pay homage to the power of hormones to engender maleness, symbolised so aptly by the cock. They tell the story of the Swedish doctor and scientist Arnold Adolph Berthold, who, through his experiments on male chickens, first demonstrated scientifically the action of a hormone – long before any had been chemically isolated. In 1849 Berthold showed that castrated male birds regained their masculine red comb, as well as their urge to crow, behave aggressively and mate, after he transplanted testicles into their abdomens. Later generations of investigators were to demonstrate that this masculine vigour was caused by the release of the hormone testosterone from the avian gonads.

How appropriate, then, that a thoroughly intact-looking cockerel, his scarlet comb resplendent, poses for the cover of a recent textbook on 'behavioural endocrinology'.[1] Modern science has revealed that the cock, ancient talisman of masculinity, has his hormones to thank for his status as king of the roost. Unveiling the mysteries of human hormones, the endocrinologists imply, will similarly reveal the chemical wellsprings of masculine sexual desire. Testosterone, the hormone men need to manufacture sperm, is also suspected of making them want to dispense it.

Doctors in the 1940s called the newly purified hormone 'medical dynamite' and 'sexual TNT',[2] but long before then, testosterone had been seen as the active principle underlying maleness, the source of masculine vigour and virility. Although the search for a 'fountain of youth' is an age-old obsession, the roots of modern concerns reach back to the summer of 1889, when a seventy-two-year-old French physiologist, Charles Edouard Brown-Séquard, startled his colleagues at the Society of Biology in Paris by announcing that he had succeeded in rejuvenating himself by injecting aqueous extracts of crushed guinea pigs' and dogs' testicles. The result, he claimed, had been a marked improvement in vigour and mental clarity. His impotence had gone, and his bladder control was much improved. He reasoned that testicles contain an active, 'dynamogenic' substance that could rejuvenate old men. 'The scientific world and the popular press greeted Brown-Séquard's report with a mixture of disbelief and enthusiasm', says the historian Merriley Borell, now at the Bakken Library in Minneapolis.[3] Within weeks, many doctors were treating their male patients with organ extracts.

Today, Brown-Séquard's results are put down to the power of the placebo effect – essentially, wishful thinking. Little of the testicular hormones would have dissolved in the water he used as his solvent. Nonetheless, his ideas were taken up with great alacrity, and not just because he was a famous scientist. His claims made sense in the light of the scientific consensus of the day.

'Organotherapy' as advocated by Brown-Séquard eventually fell into disrepute, as others failed to replicate his findings. Only extracts from the thyroid and adrenal glands had any consistent therapeutic or physiological effect. Yet the Brown-Séquard affair had convinced most medical men that bodily tissues produced 'internal secretions' that would prove therapeutic. The search was on for the substances produced by the gonads – testicles or ovaries – presumed to be essential to healthy manhood or womanhood.

The discovery of the first hormone, secretin in the intestine, in 1902 fostered the realisation that chemicals as well as nerves could have physiological effects. The English physiologists William Bayliss and Ernest Starling showed that secretin was produced by part of the small intestine to stimulate the secretion of pancreatic juice, and they coined the name 'hormone'. At about the same time, the presence of a 'female' hormone in the ovaries was confirmed by a Viennese gynaecologist, Emil Knauer, who caused young animals to sexually mature early by transplanting ovaries removed from older animals. Soon, clinicians were giving their menopausal patients dried ovaries or extracts. The Swiss drug manufacturer Ciba marketed an ovarian extract in 1913.

By 1910 no one doubted the existence of ovarian and testicular hormones, and researchers began looking for them in earnest. Physiologists supposed that once they tracked down the active ingredients secreted by testicles and ovaries, they would have discovered the essence of masculinity or femininity, and the elixir of youthful vitality and sexuality. Clinicians eagerly put these ideas into practice, and in the years immediately following the First World War the public was well aware of the prospect of rejuvenation offered by organotherapy.

The Monkey Gland Affair

For a time, Serge Voronoff, a flamboyant Paris surgeon, 'enjoyed world-wide fame for his alleged successes in rejuvenating the weary or reviving sexual appetites through the grafting of monkeys' testicles' on to his patients' own, writes David Hamilton in his entertaining account of what came to be known as the 'monkey gland affair'.[4] Across the Atlantic, the American John Brinkley also built up a lucrative private practice centred around goat-gland transplants. About twenty-five young goats were shipped in each week in the heyday of his clinic. His often distinguished patients, including leading newspaper editors and university professors, gave press conferences praising Brinkley's treatment.

Although clinicians were later to condemn these treatments – as it became clear that the animal organs were quickly rejected by their human hosts, and that Brinkley had no medical qualifications – such surgery remained in vogue for almost a decade. Leading endocrinologists were not altogether unhappy with the public interest in their subject, but some feared the disapproval of their colleagues in other fields. In 1922 the English endocrinologist Swale Vincent warned that the science of hormones was in danger of becoming disreputable, and argued that good medical practice required restraint in the prescription of extracts whose efficacy had not been demonstrated.[5]

Other endocrinologists did not share Vincent's disquiet, and used public interest in the medical treatments on offer to establish a prominent place for their young science in the medical curriculum. In popular lectures and writings, they actively encouraged the belief that human behaviour is determined by hormones. Sir Walter Langdon-Brown, professor of medicine at Cambridge, popularised the idea that we are 'marionettes of our glands'. Ernest Starling, professor of physiology at University College London, also failed to share Vincent's 'critical doubts' about the doctrine of internal secretions. The optimistic Starling enthused that it was almost too wonderful not to be true:

> It seems almost a fairy tale that such widespread results, affecting every aspect of a man's life, should be conditioned by the presence or absence in the body of infinitesimal quantities of a substance which by its formula does not seem to stand out from the thousands of other substances with which organic chemistry has made us familiar.[6]

Spain's leading endocrinologist of this period, Gregorio Marañón, also fought to enhance his subject's prestige and its legitimation as a medical speciality by pressing the theme of glandular determination of human behaviour in medical biographies of famous people, identifying Don Juan, for instance, as a 'hypergonadal' individual. In 1915 he stated that hormones 'must be regarded as moulds and guides of the biology of the individual'. He argued that the glands control sexual life, physical structure, involuntary physiological responses, the emotions, individual psychological characteristics and susceptibility to disease. In 1925 Marañón claimed that the onset of old age was directly linked to the 'cessation of hormonal activity in the genital glands'. The newspapers gave prominent coverage to the operations he performed following Voronoff's procedure – publicity which helped him to establish a firm institutional base for endocrinology in the country's medical schools. 'Popular enthusiasm for chemical determinism lent force to Marañón's position at a critical juncture,' writes historian Thomas Glick of Boston University. 'The first generation of Spanish endocrinologists not only satisfied the public's demand for an endocrinological view of human biology, but they also institutionalised that view.'[7]

The study of the endocrinology of sex was given an enormous boost by the interest of the powerful Rockefeller Foundation in the United States. Although the word 'sexology' was not invented until after the Second World War, the subject matter had already been targeted by scientists in the 1920s, according to historian Diana Long. The Committee for Research in Problems of Sex, with funding from the Rockefeller Foundation, funded scores of researchers, and by 1938 a quarter of the papers in the prestigious journal *Endocrinology* were by researchers funded by the committee. The birth of hormonal sex research also marks the beginning of research on captive primates. The need to keep monkeys and apes in laboratories for endocrine studies of the menstrual cycle – not present in other animals – was used to justify the huge expense of setting up the Yerkes Primate Laboratory, with Rockefeller funding. Studies of the reproductive hormones of our closest relatives would, Robert Yerkes argued, 'contribute to the solution of our own intensely practical medical, social and psychological problems'.[8]

The Definitive Sex Test

In the late 1920s and early 1930s, when the sex hormones were at last isolated, 'expectations were high that they would provide scientists with a tool to determine the sex of herma-phrodites and to explain the "feminine character" of homo-sexual men', writes Nelly Oudshoorn, a historian at the University of Amsterdam.[9] The 'sex' hormones would form the basis of a definitive test, revealing who was a man and who was a woman. These hormones were also expected to sort out the anomalies – people with ambiguous genitalia, for instance, or homosexuals.

The first success came in 1929, when Edward Doisy and Adolf Butenandt crystallised a 'female' sex hormone, named oestrone, from the urine of pregnant women. A related hor-mone, oestriol, was isolated from pregnant women's urine the following summer in London. These were deemed to be different sorts of 'oestrogens', the family name for female sex hormones. The name is significant, for it comes from the word 'oestrus', the time during which some female animals are said to be sexually receptive, or 'on heat'. From the beginning, the supposed elixir of womanhood was linked with sexual avail-ability, with animal passion.

A year later, Butenandt waded through 15,000 litres of men's urine to isolate the first 'androgen', or putative 'male' hormone, called androsterone. Two years later, nearly a ton of bulls' testicles yielded a few milligrams of the more potent androgen, testosterone. These male sex hormones were grouped together as androgens, as virile 'male-causing' chem-icals.

Further chemical analyses led to an unsettling discovery: both androgens and oestrogens were steroids, and chemically very similar. This was a severe blow to the deep-seated feeling that sex differences ought to be based on sex hormones that are distinctively different even in chemical terms. Worse was to follow. 'Female' sex hormones were discovered in male ani-mals. A report in *Nature* in 1934 created a stir. A Berlin gynae-cologist, Bernard Zondek, then working at the University of Stockholm, found oestrogenic hormone in the urine of the stallion. These paradoxical findings could not be dismissed. Time and again, researchers found supposedly 'female' hormones in male animals or humans, and vice versa.

By the 1940s, however, endocrinologists had taken these surprising findings on board, and adjusted their theory accordingly. They argued that maleness and femaleness were the result of a balance of hormones. Men had more of the male one, the androgens, while women more of the female ones, the oestrogens. Sex hormones were acknowledged not to be the exclusive property of one sex or the other. Yet the names androgens and oestrogens, along with the distinction 'male' and 'female' hormones, persist. So does the idea that the sex hormones are able to stimulate behaviour deemed quintessentially masculine or feminine.

Aphrodisiacs for Women?

The scene is set for the contradictions in both scientific research and clinical practice. On the face of it, the sexuality of women might be expected to lie in the action of the 'female' hormones. High levels of oestrogens should fuel feminine desire. Yet it is men, not women, who are regarded as sexually active. So the hormonal wellsprings of sexual desire seem more readily linked to 'male' testosterone than to 'female' oestrogen.

This, then, is the quandary: how do we account for the observation that women, too, can experience sexual desire? Could it be that testosterone fuels sexual desire in women too? But to reach that conclusion entails explicitly crossing the boundary between the hormonally distinguished sexes. It also has implications for the hormonal treatments available to women in the form of contraception and 'hormone replacement therapy' (HRT). Neither oral contraceptives nor HRT typically contains testosterone supplements. Rich in oestrogen, they are designed to enhance feminine qualities valued by men: the contraceptive Pill is intended to make women more sexually available; HRT to maintain their desirability. Scientists and clinicians in this field grapple with these contradictions. Research findings are inconsistent; clinical practice is varied.

Can giving testosterone to women raise their libido? Alan Riley, a leading British sexologist, argues: 'there can be no doubt that in clinical practice androgen therapy can improve sexual desire and function'.[10] Yet he adds that the hard evidence for this confidence is lacking: 'the results of controlled clinical trials have been less convincing'.

However, Raymond Goodman, consultant in psychosexual medicine in Manchester, is a firm believer in the value of testosterone treatment for women.[11] He tells the story of one patient in her mid forties, with four children. She told her GP that after their third child she had lost all desire to have sex with her husband. Three years later her husband was disgruntled, and the marriage was breaking up. The woman pleaded with the doctor to do something. 'It's my fault the marriage is on the rocks,' she said. 'I've denied him, and of course he's got other women.' The doctor gave her an injection of testosterone on the Monday. 'On Thursday the husband phoned, and asked, could I lower the dose? – it had been that effective.' Goodman claims that one or two injections of testosterone every six months 'is one of the most useful drugs for women with low libido'.

Another British sexologist, John Kellett, consultant psychiatrist at St George's Hospital in London, recalls a woman he treated for low libido. To test the efficacy of the hormone, she agreed to be treated 'blind' – no one knew whether the injection she had was testosterone or a harmless but useless substance, a placebo. 'Two hours after the injection she had a spontaneous orgasm. She and her husband made love five times the first week, three times the next.' Then the effect wore off, and she returned for another injection. 'We broke the code and discovered she had been given the placebo.' After her next injection – of the real stuff – nothing happened. 'It shows how careful you have to be in this business,' says Kellett. When it comes to human sexual desire, few things are as powerful as the power of suggestion.[12]

It is 'a very difficult and demanding field of study', opines Sue Carter, an endocrinologist at the University of Maryland who has made a special study of the sexuality of female golden hamsters and prairie voles. The sex steroids 'do not seem to affect sexual behavior in humans or other primates as clearly or as strongly as they do in rodents'.[13]

Does Anticipation Boost Your Hormones?

Nonetheless, heroic attempts to link hormones and desire continue. One recent study, inspired by new techniques that allow researchers to measure free testosterone in a teaspoon of saliva, looked for a short-term link between testosterone and sex. Two psychologists at the Georgia State University in Atlanta convinced four established heterosexual couples in their twenties to volunteer to donate their saliva for science.[14] The researchers thoughtfully gave the couples chewing gum to make things easier. Thus equipped, the volunteers collected, over eight days, one saliva sample after they had eaten dinner, and another before going to sleep. They were asked to mark on the pre-sleep sample whether they had made love in the interval between food and sleep.

The psychologists report problems in data collection. Some subjects forgot to collect samples, or neglected to put them in the freezer. Others had sexual intercourse every evening or at the wrong time in the evening (before they had collected their first saliva sample), or not at all. Eventually, however, the researchers managed to collect samples from each subject over three sex and three non-sex days.

To the researchers' dismay, early-evening hormone levels did not differ on the sex and non-sex days – so discrediting the notion that higher testosterone levels enhance sexual interest and make sexual intercourse more probable. The psychologists found only that once the subjects had made love, testosterone levels in both men and women were higher than they had been earlier in the evening. This finding is none too exciting, given that running round the block or similar bursts of exercise are known to raise testosterone levels for a brief time in both sexes.

Sex Survives Castration

Castration has long been regarded as an effective punishment for male sex offenders, and as a prerequisite for the job of harem keeper. Yet castrated men can have erections and orgasms. People of either sex who have very low levels of the typical sex hormones can easily progress through all the stages of human sexual response meticulously documented in the 1960s by the American sexologists William Masters and Virginia Johnson. Moreover, men in their eighties may remain sexually active, even though testosterone levels begin to decline at around fifty and drop markedly after the age of sixty.

So much is agreed by most commentators on human sexuality.[15] But many sexologists – Carter for one – are convinced that sex steroids may still 'modulate' human sexuality, or even 'enhance sexual motivation' – the desire for a sexual encounter. The best evidence for this idea comes from a few men with a rare genetic condition, Kallman's syndrome. These men do not produce enough of a hormone (called gonadotrophin-releasing hormone, or GnRH) that normally stimulates the testicles to produce testosterone. So they do not develop the body hair, deep voice and enlarged testicles normally associated with puberty in boys, and remain youthful in appearance, unless they are given the missing hormone GnRH artificially. Carter reports that untreated men with this condition are not usually homosexual. But, she claims, they are relatively uninterested in sex, and mildly depressed. Clinicians have given these men hormone replacement therapy, and charted their progress. A few months later, the patients reported that they were more keen on the idea of sexual encounters, and experienced spontaneous erections more frequently. But even after a year of the hormonal treatment, Carter tells us, the men did not masturbate or have sex more than before.

Men whose testicles produce unusually low levels of testosterone for some other reason have also come under the gaze of the sexologists. These so-called hypogonadal men appear to be as likely as the next man to produce erections in the laboratory in response to erotic stimulation such as pornography or personal fantasies.[16] Perhaps, the researchers conclude, the testosterone naturally produced by the adrenal glands and fat tissue (in both men and women) is sufficient to fuel sexual desire. If this supply is enough to make up for castration, it suggests that men need very little to lead an active sex life.

Do Hormones Foster Fantasy Life?

Backed into a corner, sex specialists now argue that testosterone can stimulate one aspect of human sexuality variously described as spontaneous sexual thoughts, sexual desire, sexual interest or libido. It is these spontaneous sexual thoughts that are claimed to increase among hypogonadal men, in response to androgen treatments.

'This hypothesis is, of course, very difficult to test,' Carter agrees. 'The occurrence of a "thought" is subject to many non-hormonal processes including experience.' She proceeds to put her finger on a probable explanation for many of these results: 'the very act of requesting information could alter an individual's frequency of sex-related thoughts'.

A recent attempt to get round the problem of having to rely on men's own accounts of their sexual feelings and activities has also failed to show that testosterone is the ultimate aphrodisiac. In an effort to link testosterone and libido, Gerianne Alexander and Barbara Sherwin of McGill University in Montreal turned to an ingenious psychological test, based on the principle of 'selective interference'.[17] The idea is that an individual's ability to concentrate on one task while being distracted by another will vary, depending on how attention-grabbing the distraction is. The psychologists asked men to repeat aloud the 'target message' played into one ear. The men were meant to ignore a distracting message played into the other: neutral information about wildlife, the weather or travel, or sexual passages taken from D.H. Lawrence's *Lady Chatterley's Lover* or Anaïs Nin's *Delta of Venus*, describing kissing, genital fondling and oral-genital contact.

The researchers predicted that the higher the man's testosterone level, the more he would be distracted by the erotic material. They expected that the high-testosterone men would have more trouble concentrating on the target message they were supposed to repeat, and would make more mistakes than those burdened with less testosterone. But no relationship was found between hormones and distractibility by the erotic tape recording.

In all these attempts to link hormones and desire, confounding factors abound. For instance, testosterone could enhance sexual desire through its wide-ranging anabolic effects, improving feelings of well-being and so enhancing sexual behaviour as a side-effect, as the pioneering Alfred Kinsey and his colleagues argued in the 1950s. 'Mood questionnaires' suggest that hypogonadal men with low androgen levels may feel lethargic and depressed. It is equally plausible that simply being under medical treatment makes people feel better, and so enhances sexual feelings.

One finding about testosterone and sex is in a class of its own – the claim that hypogonadal men receiving androgen treatment over many months progressively become less sensitive to a vibrator applied to their penis or finger. The researchers who did this work had expected higher levels of testosterone to make men *more* sensitive to touch (and thus more enthusiastic about sexual pleasures), not less, as it turned out. The researchers are at a loss to explain these findings.[18]

So, despite repeated attempts, no one has found a compelling link between sexual behaviour and testosterone levels in men in the normal range. John Bancroft, a leading researcher in sexual endocrinology at the Medical Research Council's Reproductive Biology Unit in Edinburgh, tries to explain this by proposing that most men produce far more testosterone than is needed to support sexual behaviour. He suggests that there is a threshold level of circulating testosterone needed for male sexuality, which happens to lie at the bottom of the normal range.[19] Exceed this level and nothing happens, he speculates. Bancroft cheerfully admits that there is no evidence to support his idea. Nonetheless, it allows sexologists to preserve a role for testosterone in maintaining male sexual interest, despite the tenuous evidence.

The Quest for the Elixir of Female Desire

Many specialists suspect that in women, too, testosterone – produced by the ovaries and the adrenal glands – is linked to interest in sex. This is an intriguing hypothesis, given that women produce substantially less testosterone than men do. Researchers have nimbly skirted round this stumbling block by suggesting that women could actually be more sensitive than men to the behavioural effects of androgens.

One recent study is unusual only in the thoroughness with which the researchers tried to relate hormone levels to differences in female sexual desire. Patricia Schreiner-Engel and her colleagues at the Mount Sinai School of Medicine in New York compared two groups of healthy women.[20] One group complained of 'a persistent, pervasive and severe lack of sexual desire'; the other had an active heterosexual sex life. Despite measuring blood levels of six different hormones, including testosterone, the researchers could find no significant differences between the women in the two groups.

Undaunted, researchers have tried another tack. Women, in common with the females of many of our primate relatives, are renowned for their ability to indulge in sexual activity whenever they see fit – most primates are not restricted to being sexual in just one phase of their reproductive cycle. Even so, if women could be shown to have sex more often at certain times of the month, the timing of the peaks in sexual activity could perhaps reveal which hormones turn on libido – with testosterone as the prime candidate.

To explore this issue, Bancroft asked many women, heterosexual and lesbian alike, to chart their sexual thoughts and activity over several months. Despite finding substantial individual differences, he concluded that the most common times for peaks of sexual interest are the weeks before and after menstruation.[21] This is an awkward finding, because testosterone varies through the menstrual cycle, with the highest levels generally at mid cycle, around ovulation. Bancroft's studies, and several others, suggest that sexual interest and activity are likely to be at their lowest at this time. Yet other researchers claim that women are more sexually active at mid cycle, when oestrogen levels are highest.[22] Meanwhile, in another study, Bancroft has linked testosterone levels in women not with interest in sexual intercourse, but with the frequency of masturbation. Bancroft has come up with an explanation for these contradictory findings. He argues that women suffer from a conflict between the different behavioural effects of hormones. Men, in Bancroft's account, have it easy: testosterone makes a man 'more sexy, more muscular and possibly more assertive – in other words, more "masculine" in conventional terms'. But pity the poor woman. 'Some women may be made more sexy by androgens,' Bancroft argues, 'but also more career-orientated or assertive and less prepared to conform with the expectations of their traditional husbands and society.'

According to Bancroft, such women are burdened with a sexual desire that is at odds with their feminine role. This may explain, he says, his finding that at mid cycle some women were more keen to masturbate but less keen to have sexual intercourse. This conflict may even drive some of them to become lesbians, Bancroft speculates: 'If such conflicts do occur it would not be surprising to find some women with higher testosterone levels adopting a homosexual lifestyle where the combination of sexiness and "non-conformity" would cause no conflict.'[23]

Lesbians have not been found to have consistently higher testosterone levels than heterosexual women, and are consistently reported, on average, to have sex less, not more, frequently than either heterosexual couples or gay men. So to substantiate his theory, Bancroft cites a study of the testosterone levels of women in different sorts of employment.[24] Frances Purifoy, an anthropologist, and Lambert Koopmans, a statistician, reported in 1980 that women who were students or in professional and managerial jobs tended to have higher levels than those who were clerical workers, service workers or housewives. Interestingly, the researchers did not conclude that women in the higher-status jobs got there because of their testosterone. Rather, they saw the variation in hormone level as the result of different levels of stress. The women stuck at home or in traditional low-status women's jobs had more symptoms of stress (such as insomnia, headaches, depression and anxiety) than those in well-paid employment; and it is well established that stress can lower testosterone levels.

A later survey of heterosexual college students by Bancroft, Sherwin, and their colleagues failed to find any relationship between women's testosterone levels and their sexual activities, or their satisfaction with their male partners.[25]

Ingredients for Women's Hormonal 'Therapy'?

Oral contraceptives dose women with oestrogen and artificial versions of progesterone, crudely mimicking the hormonal profile during pregnancy. Depression and loss of libido are acknowledged to be possible side-effects, but gynaecologists are reluctant to attribute either of these to the contraceptive Pill itself. Popular handbooks written by doctors are filled with helpful suggestions about thinking positively and seeking psychosexual counselling,[26] but they also suggest that a woman might try transferring to a more oestrogen-dominant formulation, or one containing a new-type synthetic progestogen. Oestrogen is seen as sex-promoting, progesterone as a turn-off, but there is no suggestion that testosterone deficiency might be the root of the trouble – even though oral contraceptives are acknowledged to lower women's testosterone levels.[27]

Perhaps testosterone is not advocated for women of reproductive age because prolonged treatment is deemed to carry the risk of significant side-effects, including infertility, male patterns of body-hair growth, deepening of voice, baldness, and damage to liver and the cardiovascular system.[28] These side-effects are not seen as insuperable problems for older women, however, and some clinicians argue the case for adding testosterone supplements to hormonal therapy. Yet medical opinion varies widely.

Studies of women taking hormones have yielded contradictory results.[29] One study found that oestrogen, and oestrogen and testosterone together, are equally good at improving sexual satisfaction, desire, arousal and frequency of orgasm in

27

postmenopausal women. Another reported that oestrogen or oestrogen–progestogen combinations were better than progestogen alone, or a placebo; while yet others conclude that adding progestogen reduces the benefits of oestrogen. The British gynaecologist John Studd argues that oestrogen improves sexual satisfaction only in women who suffer pain during intercourse due to vaginal dryness. He claims that sexual desire is enhanced only by adding testosterone to the oestrogen pill.[30] Meanwhile, most women on HRT are given oestrogen alone, or a mixture of oestrogen and progestogen, and it is routinely claimed that the treatment revitalises a woman's sex life, whatever the hormonal mix.

As Germaine Greer points out, some of these interventions treat the woman for her male partner's sake.[31] It is as if the contraceptive pills or hormone replacement treatments are designed to maximise a male partner's sexual pleasure. But Greer sees giving testosterone to women as particularly problematic, interestingly, because she too sees it as a 'male' hormone. In *The Change* she writes:

> When we give a male hormone to a married woman who has lost interest in sex, we are consciously tailoring her sexuality to fit her husband's; the whole business smacks of women's willingness to try anything for a quiet life ... The medicalization of everyday life is here taken to its absurd extreme. The husband has become the wife's health problem, and testosterone in her body the treatment for him.

Perhaps no hormonal mixture is clearly for the woman herself – but rather, for some conception of what it is to be hormonally feminine. Overall, testosterone for women may be seen as too risky – not because it might damage their health, but because it threatens the gender distinctions which some scientists still seek to ground in biological difference.

Gail Sheehy, journalist and author of a bestselling book on the menopause, *The Silent Passage*, adds a new twist to testosterone in the menopausal woman.[32] She implies that it is responsible for what she calls 'postmenopausal zest': 'greater assertiveness' and a resurgence of sexual desire apparently

28

experienced by some older women. One of the experts she interviewed, a psychoanalyst, suggests that this testosterone-inspired boost to sexual urges prompts some women who have impotent husbands, or are widowed or divorced, to 'turn to homosexual relationships with other women when they had never considered that before'. But the amazing powers attributed to testosterone in the menopausal woman cannot be linked to any rise in testosterone levels – which, in fact, decline by a third or more. Sheehy thinks of testosterone and oestrogen as opposing forces, pushing us in masculine or feminine directions. Because oestrogen levels fall even more dramatically, she reasons that what she calls the testosterone 'chaser' is no longer so effectively cancelled out by oestrogen as it was before menopause. She seems to think of these hormones as 'male' and 'female' principles, and that the balance between these two essences determines how we behave. Physiological evidence for this unusual hypothesis seems lacking – sex hormones do not appear to work in conflict with one another – yet the idea is appealing because it fits so well with the common belief that masculinity and femininity are opposites.

Yet later in her book, Sheehy emphasises the fall in testosterone levels to account for the observation that some women find 'their sexual pilot light abruptly lowered'. These women may need testosterone treatment, she says. But her medical informants stress that they give 'very small' dosages or 'very weak' forms of testosterone which avoid any visible masculinising effects, yet nonetheless produce, they claim, a 'subtle return of sexual vitality'.

The Lure of Hormonal Explanations

Although concerns around gender divisions help to shape current attitudes and practices surrounding the medical and scientific study of desire, there are many other reasons why some people are drawn to hormonally framed explanations. The paedophile who escapes a life sentence by volunteering to undergo chemical castration, for instance, clearly has a vested interest in finding a chemical origin for his situation. One man in this predicament fought to stay on the hormone-blocking drug goserelin, manufactured by ICI for the treatment of prostate cancer.[33] The journalist reporting the story commented: 'The paucity of research in the field means there is little evidence about which treatments work and which don't.' But the judge in the case had no doubts: 'The safety of generations of children to come depends on whether one can find a sympathetic psychiatrist to give this treatment.'

Similarly, the so-called 'M4 rapist' claimed in his trial in 1986 that the steroids (testosterone derivatives) he injected as a bodybuilder gave him 'an uncontrollable sexual appetite'. Scotland Yard's Forensic Department is apparently now 'examining the evidence' linking anabolic steroid abuse with violent sex attacks.[34]

People suffering from sexual difficulties of one kind or another may also welcome biological explanations for their problems. Indeed, a battle is under way for the hearts and minds of sex therapists, and there is every sign that 'organogenic (or biogenic) diagnoses of sexual disorders will grow at the expense of those which are psychogenic', concludes Martin Cole, a British sex therapist.[35]

Yet there remain other reasons for the enduring appeal of hormonal accounts of libido, beyond the desire to avoid a prison sentence or a psychotherapist. Scientific and medical conceptions of hormones reveal much about the cultural preoccupations of our time.

Hormonal explanations of desire presuppose that desire is something inside us – a force unleashed by a surge of hormones. So powerful is this idea that it may seem odd to argue that sexuality is about relationships between people, who act in ways which have meaning, and that desire is typically manifested as desire for intimate connection with some particular person. The way in which simplistic hormonal accounts of human behaviour push human agency and the social context of our lives out of the picture is a persistent theme.

The 'Cuddle Chemical'

A good example comes from recent research on the hormone oxytocin. Sue Carter takes a particular interest in oxytocin as a hormonal player in the orgasmic phase of sex. This interesting little peptide, a protein fragment secreted by the pituitary gland, is good at making smooth muscles contract – for instance, it stimulates the contraction of the uterus at birth, and the release of milk from a mother's breasts. It is also released during orgasm, prompting the penis to ejaculate and the vagina to contract. This link between oxytocin and orgasm has inspired Carter to hope for greater things for the hormone. She suggests that the oxytocin released during orgasm acts on the central nervous system to induce a 'refractory state' – an inability to become sexually aroused again immediately – and feelings of 'sexual satiety' – 'I've had enough'. In sheep, but not in rats, oxytocin also seems to help to orchestrate a mother's recognition of her young. In one of those glorious scientific statements of awesome naivety, Carter goes on: 'Shared sexual experience may thereby facilitate social bond formation in humans.'[36]

The idea that our desire to form meaningful relationships with others could be attributed to a hormone or two has been taken up by the popular press. Timed for Valentine's Day 1993, *Time* magazine's cover was devoted to 'The Chemistry of Love', with the cover line 'Scientists are discovering that romance is a biological affair'. *Time*'s journalists call oxytocin the 'cuddle chemical', and report that it 'produces feelings of attachment'.[37]

In the 1970s, oxytocin was commonly regarded as the probable source of a mother's love for her newborn baby, writes Diane Eyer, a psychologist at the University of Pennsylvania, in her recent book *Mother–Infant Bonding: A Scientific Fiction*.[38] Two American paediatricians, John Kennell and Marshall Klaus, were intrigued by animal studies which established that female goats and sheep reject their young if they are separated for as little as five minutes after birth. In sheep, oxytocin released at birth forms part of a neuroendocrine pathway that enables the mother ewe very rapidly to learn to distinguish her lamb by smell from all the others – so safe-guarding her from being inundated by newborn lambs eager to suckle.[39] Kennell and Klaus reasoned that the same thing might be happening in women. Their influential book *Maternal–Infant Bonding*, published in 1976, claimed to have discovered a hormonally driven 'critical period' after birth during which mothers must 'bond' with their babies.[40] Although Kennell and Klaus did not measure women's hormone levels, and had only poorly controlled comparisons between women who had differed in their contact with their newborn babies for all sorts of reasons, the theory was widely applauded: it seemed to provide a biological explanation for child abuse that avoided any need to consider poverty and social disadvantage, and supported the conservative claim that mothers should not work outside the home. Yet human mothers have turned out to be distinctly different from ewes, and it is now generally acknowledged that the bonding theory is seriously flawed.

Kennell and Klaus still believe, however, that new studies with sophisticated hormonal monitoring techniques will eventually vindicate their theory. The enduring appeal of the notion that a mother is locked to her infant, chemically bonded through the adhesive action of some molecular glue, stems from the fact that it fits so well with some people's notions of what motherhood should be. Feminist childbirth reformers, in contrast, continue to argue that 'the problems of birth are the dehumanising practices of hospitals – not some phenomenon within women', as Eyer points out. Maternal–infant bonding is not a passing fad, she concludes. It persists as an explanation of mother love because we have no adequate means of dealing with the social and political forces inherent in research.

2

HORMONAL TIMES

BLOOD, 'BAD' BEHAVIOUR
AND BIORHYTHMS

The British doctor who made 'premenstrual syndrome' a household name, Katharina Dalton, argues that the premenstrual woman can wreak havoc in her household:

> One survey showed that the husband's late arrival at work was a reflection of the time of his wife's cycle. They both failed to get up with the alarm, they quarrelled over breakfast which consequently took longer, and then the sandwiches weren't ready![1]

Instability and unpredictability have long been considered the hallmark of female physiology. Male hormones are seen as constant, reliable, generally unproblematic. On the face of it, a simple fact of biology seems to account for contrasting images of masculinity and femininity. Men produce sperm all the time; women produce a single egg once a month. Men do not get pregnant; women do. So in women the hormones that orchestrate the reproductive system must change in a cyclical fashion – first to allow the release of a mature egg, and then to set the stage for a potential pregnancy. Yet biological difference cannot explain why these cyclical hormonal changes are given such significance.

There is a paradox here. The menstrual cycle is seen as defining the tangible essence of womanhood. The onset of menstruation in adolescence roughly coincides with the beginning of fertility; its cessation at the menopause is seen as a sign of the loss of feminine allure. Yet the menstrual cycle is also regarded as the private concern of individual women. The roots of this paradox reveal much about the way both male and female bodies are perceived and 'managed' in Western culture today.

Because femininity is so closely linked with the monthly ovarian cycle, women are defined as experiencing another time, at odds with the public, objective time. Women are expected to manage their own cycles within that public time, by and large without acknowledgement of their experience of difference. This disjuncture is seen as a private matter for the individual to deal with as best she can. From her research at the University of Warwick, Sophie Laws speaks of a 'menstrual etiquette' which dictates that women should behave in public life as if monthly cyclical changes do not happen.[2]

Successful womanhood entails the management of these cycles, so that they do not 'get in the way' – do not inconvenience other people.[3] School is the first major public context in which most girls will learn about menstruation, as Shirley Prendergast of the University of Cambridge illustrated in her recent study of adolescent girls' experiences. One fifth-year student said of her experience of periods: 'It's much better now, you learn all the things to do, you get to know how to keep it to yourself. Use the right toilets, get home at the right time, all that.'

These cycles become cause for comment and concern when this management breaks down, or when the cycles themselves seem irregular, out of control. The aim of medical treatment is to 'get the woman regular'. Another fifth-year student in Prendergast's study expressed her anxiety about menstruating irregularly:

My periods are so irregular, and I have to keep going to the doctor. And there's a terrible feeling that you think that they think that you are pregnant. And my mum says, you know, well that didn't happen to me, so why does it happen to you?

Yet it is acknowledged that both sexes have bodily rhythms in body temperature and in the levels of most hormones – cycles that are purported to be controlled by inner 'biological clocks'. But in men these cycles are rarely spoken of, or seen as grounds for concern. Nor does the idea of a mismatch between public and personal time sit well as a concept applied to men, the archetypal definers of what is public space and time.

Specialists in the infant field of chronobiology are now working hard to establish the importance of their work. They say they can predict times of optimal performance and maximum efficiency, and may yet find ways of resetting people's clocks. Researchers seek cures for jet lag and treatments for tired, inefficient shift workers. Even mental illness, many chronobiologists claim, may result from disruptions to the body's inner rhythms, putting individuals 'out of sync' with the world. The patient's disordered, unpredictable behaviour is increasingly attributed to chaotic inner timekeeping. Yet researchers have so far failed to reveal the mechanisms of the 'master' clock purported to be in charge of it all. Effective treatments to jolt individuals back into synchrony have also proved elusive.

Chronobiology's theoretical problems – notably its failure to find the 'clock' – may lie in the presumption that there are individual rhythms which are independent of social context. What is perceived to be inherent in the individual – the inner presentation of the rhythm – may be more fruitfully regarded as a dynamic relationship with the world. From this perspective, it becomes evident that in contemporary culture the construction and perception of biological time are intimately linked to gender.

Once a Month: Female Cycles and Premenstrual Syndrome

'Sex hormones' became defined by the means of their discovery, Nelly Oudshoorn has argued.[4] Scientists could isolate them from thousands of litres of urine only because they had 'bioassays' that told them whether one partially purified sample had more of the active ingredient than another. These bioassays consisted of living animals, or freshly dissected organs, which respond in a measurable way to the amount of hormone to which they are exposed. The label 'female sex hormones' was attached to chemicals that stimulate the growth of a rat's uterus and the development of scaly-looking cells in the lining of her vagina when she is 'on heat', or in oestrus. Scientists can easily detect these cells by looking at a rat's vaginal smear under the microscope. So, from the beginning, 'oestrogens' became linked to the rat's oestrus cycle, and identified with cyclicity in the female. The word 'oestrus' itself comes from the Latin for 'gadfly' – hence 'that which causes a frenzy'.

Today, these cyclical changes are said to inflict 'chaos' on a million British homes every month, according to Katharina Dalton. They can drive women to baby-battering, alcoholism, shoplifting and homicide and thus, by Dalton's reckoning, rank as one of the greatest public health issues of our time.[5] Dalton has been 'an expert witness in three murder trials and two of infanticide', the first in 1979, in which premenstrual syndrome was accepted as a factor causing diminished responsibility, 'thus making legal history in Britain', says the blurb on her best-selling book *Once a Month*. In one well-publicised case, Christine English used her car to crush her former lover against a telegraph pole. In another, Sandra Craddock was charged with killing another barmaid at work. Both pleas to manslaughter were accepted on grounds of premenstrual syndrome. English received a conditional discharge and a driving ban; Craddock received progesterone therapy and a probation order.

Barrister Helena Kennedy believes that cases of a profoundly disturbed hormonal balance are 'extremely rare' –

she says she has come across only one case in her practice where she felt it justified to argue that premenstrual syndrome be taken into account as a mitigating factor.[6] But Dalton argues that many women suffer from pronounced hormonal imbalances. Prejudice and medical ignorance exacerbate the suffering of millions of women. To the husband who pleads: 'Tell me, Doctor, why does my wonderful wife, with her perfect figure and lovely nature, suddenly spit with rage for no obvious reason once a month?', Dr Dalton replies that the answer lies in the 'ebb and flow of the menstrual hormones over which the woman has such little control'. She warns husbands to keep tabs on their wives. 'If she has a taste for alcohol, she may well have uncontrollable alcohol urges during this time, so keep an eye on the home supplies and if they are going down too rapidly remove all alcohol from the house. Explain to the children that Mother is not well today.'

Dalton has campaigned since the 1950s for the recognition of premenstrual syndrome (also known as premenstrual tension) as a serious medical condition, and has undoubtedly helped a great many women. She published the first paper on the subject to appear in a British medical journal in 1953, and established the world's first premenstrual syndrome clinic at University College Hospital, London. She stresses the importance of precise diagnosis, through women's careful charting of their symptoms over several months. To qualify as premenstrual syndrome, Dalton asserts, the symptoms must have appeared every month for at least three months, must happen just before menstruation, and must be absent for at least seven days after a period.

But even these diagnostic criteria have not cleared away the confusion surrounding the syndrome. A bewildering array of reported experiences, varying enormously from individual to individual, make it difficult to pin down a symptom to a particular hormone. More than 150 symptoms have been implicated, including headaches, epilepsy, dizziness, asthma, irritability, anger, anxiety, depression, loss of co-ordination, hoarseness, nausea, muscle or joint pains, heart palpitations, skin disorders, breast tenderness, conjunctivitis, memory loss, failure of concentration, loss of self-esteem, inadequate coping and changed self-concept. 'Women have complained of midnight disinfecting sprees, absent-mindedly buying basset hounds, forcing boyfriends to hold torches at night while they weed the garden, as well as the more usual tears and carving knife scenarios,' writes Helen Fielding, tongue in cheek, in *The Sunday Times*.[7] Dalton has even linked premenstrual syndrome to postnatal depression and postmenopausal problems – all are seen as the result of 'hormonal imbalance'. Yet other researchers have found remarkably little consistent variation throughout the cycle in anxiety, hostility or depression, as measured by psychological tests.

There are even more perplexing conundrums: the purported symptoms of premenstrual syndrome do not coincide with any particular pattern of hormones. Testosterone, reputed to make female monkeys more aggressive at times, reaches its highest levels in women during ovulation – supposedly the most peaceful time of the cycle. Oestrogen levels rise sharply just before ovulation, drop, then rise again during the so-called luteal phase, only to drop again before menstruation starts. Progesterone rises after ovulation, and falls along with oestrogen before bleeding begins. Dalton suggests that premenstrual syndrome can be caused by a lack of progesterone in the second half of the cycle. She recommends progesterone injections or suppositories. Other medical authorities dispute both her theory and her treatment. As one review of the evidence concludes: 'The therapeutic value of progesterone in reducing irritability and aggressiveness in women is doubtful.'[8]

Most contemporary specialists in premenstrual syndrome agree with Doreen Asso, a psychologist at the University of London, that 'there has been no demonstration of a direct relationship between individual levels of ovarian and pituitary hormones on the one hand, and mood and behaviour on the other'.[9]

Gwyneth Sampson, a psychiatrist in Sheffield specialising in premenstrual syndrome, writes in a similar vein: 'It is difficult to state that there is a consistently detectable hormonal abnormality differentiating women with PMS from other women.'[10] According to Sampson, we have not moved much beyond the pronouncements of the endocrinologist Robert Frank, who invented the term premenstrual tension and claimed in 1931 that 'excessive amounts of female sex hormone' in 'labile persons' may produce 'psychic and nervous' changes.

The origins of the premenstrual syndrome remain 'obscure', concludes another clinical endocrinologist.[11] What has become clear, he remarks, is that 'there is no known hormone which is grossly abnormal in this condition'. If there is a basic endocrine cause, it must be 'a subtle abnormality in a hormone or group of hormones which is not recognised in the weekly or daily samples of serum [blood] that have been employed in most investigations'. Dalton has tried to salvage her progesterone-deficiency theory by claiming that premenstrual syndrome is caused not by a lack of the hormone in the blood, but by something amiss in the progesterone receptors on cells in the brain. Yet there is no evidence to support this theory either.

One finding to emerge from all this speculation may be significant: the observation that there is a 'high placebo response' in many controlled treatment studies of premenstrual syndrome. No one has done any long-term studies, but women given courses of treatment that consisted of harmless but inactive substances often showed marked improvements in both their physical and mental symptoms, at least over the next cycle or two. But this does not mean that premenstrual syndrome is 'all in women's minds'. The placebo effect simply reaffirms that bodies and minds are intimately intertwined, and what anyone thinks about what is – or might be – happening to them physically can be of considerable consequence. Receiving a placebo probably itself alters endocrine profiles – a possibility Sampson considers well worth researching.

Several researchers have tried to investigate the links between a woman's experience of premenstrual symptoms and her life experiences in general. A few studies have reported that women who seek medical help for premenstrual syndrome are more likely to report conflicts within their marriage, or to feel inadequate as wife and mother. Some researchers have suggested that stressful life events predispose women to suffer premenstrually. Others have argued that women who complain of premenstrual distress are more anxious or more neurotic, have lower self-esteem and feel less in control of their lives, than women who do not report menstrual problems.

Others have advocated psychotherapy for some women with premenstrual syndrome. Two Australian psychiatrists, Carol Morse and Lorraine Dennerstein of the University of Melbourne, claim that 'cognitive therapy' can teach women new techniques of managing thoughts and emotions, and so enable them to 'experience more control'.[12] They report the plight of 'Patricia', a thirty-five-year-old divorced mother of two, who works full-time as a secretary, has a live-in lover who abdicates responsibility, and an ex-husband who ignores the children. After sessions with a psychotherapist who aimed to teach her 'more appropriate self-enhancing thinking and actions', Patricia reportedly 'felt better about herself, and her symptoms abated' as she 'increasingly took charge of her personal and interpersonal environments'. Yet this therapeutic approach can foster the notion that PMS is a woman's fault, the result of her 'irrational' or 'negative' thinking.

As Ellen Goudsmit points out, it is just as likely that premenstrual symptoms make women more anxious and lower their self-esteem.[13] Moreover, there are many other factors, apart from personality, that compromise a woman's ability to cope, including how many and how severe the stressors are, 'the absence of social support, dissatisfaction with work and home life, the existence of menstrual taboos and social disapproval of cycle-related conditions'. Several studies have also shown that a great many women who experience premenstrual distress are not psychologically unusual.

Tellingly, most of the sufferers discussed in the published literature are married, and many are working at home caring for children. 'Such a lifestyle, with its inescapable commitments, may make cyclical changes in mood and well-being less easy to tolerate, while also aggravating symptoms like irritability and fatigue,' says Goudsmit. Few studies have tried to investigate such interactions over the long term.

Another possibility, argues Goudsmit, is that expectations, attitudes and beliefs can strongly influence what women experience; unfortunately, the inconsistencies of the studies to date make it very difficult to draw any conclusions. There is, however, 'much support for the multifactorial psychosomatic models' which attempt – crudely, so far – to allow different causal mechanisms – physical, psychological and social – to interact. But we still know next to nothing about the impact of social and cultural factors on a woman's experience of menstruation.

In the circumstances, a healthy scepticism about the therapies on offer seems wise. The current medical treatments entail either destroying ('ablating') a woman's cycle, chemically or surgically, in the hopes that removing the cyclical nature of hormonal changes will remove whatever is causing the problems, or giving a large dose of some hormone, usually progesterone, presumed to be deficient during part of the cycle. Neither approach is notably successful; hence the medical acknowledgement that 'little is understood'.

Pioneering feminist self-help books such as *Why Suffer? Periods and Their Problems*, by Lynda Birke and Katy Gardner, have been torn between a desire to affirm women's experiences and to ensure that they are taken seriously by the medical profession, and a reluctance to 'medicalise' women's lives.[14] They encourage women to explore alternatives to medical treatment, and suggest that they alter their diets, form consciousness-raising groups, and take more exercise.

Yet it remains difficult for women to avoid being defined in medical terms. Early in this century, clinicians considered women who complained of menstrual disorders to be simply neurotic. The women's health movement campaigned for the recognition that their experiences were rooted in the body and its physiological changes in particular social contexts. The medical profession responded by finding simplistic hormonal explanations that required doctor-supervised cures.[15] As with the HRT debate, the alacrity with which clinicians diagnose women as somehow 'naturally abnormal' is disturbing. The focus on premenstrual syndrome, to the neglect of other aspects such as menstrual pain, may also be significant. As Sophie Laws argues, it avoids 'reference to menstrual blood, the object of male disgust, and focuses on those intangible forces, hormones, and their control over women'.[16]

Cycles of Incapacity

But premenstrual syndrome is not the only topic on the research agenda. The menstrual cycle as a whole is a perfect hunting ground for behavioural endocrinologists, because it is an ideal opportunity to nail a behaviour to a hormonal cause. Many studies have attempted – without much success – to tie sexual desire down to one or two phases of the menstrual cycle (see Chapter 1). But apparent cycles in cravings for food have also been reported. In a typical study, psychologist Barbara Sherwin and her colleagues at McGill University report that women undergraduates ate more and craved certain sweet or fatty foods during the ten days before menstruation (the luteal phase) than they did during the ten days after their period.[17] Metabolic rate appears to be slightly higher after ovulation – apparently the result of increased progesterone levels.[18]

But the undergraduates' self-reported cravings careered up and down within both phases, making it impossible to say that a particular hormone profile prompted them to eat a particular sort of food (or even how much they really did eat). The students shared the popular belief that some women crave 'forbidden' foods such as chocolate on premenstrual days; Sherwin and her colleagues even remark that the undergraduates 'seemed to enjoy communicating about their cravings and some provided richly detailed reports'.

Other psychologists, most notably Doreen Kimura of the University of Western Ontario, have looked for cyclical changes in the way women score on various tests of perception, motor skills and spatial ability. Many researchers have failed to find any significant variations, but Kimura claims some success. She says that women excel at spatial tasks when oestrogen levels are low – during and immediately after menstruation.[19] They were better, for instance, in tests asking them to pick out a familiar shape embedded in a field of other shapes – a skill Kimura says may be equivalent to finding one's own car in a large, full car park. (One Ontario newspaper reported Kimura's findings with a headline urging men not to let women park the car at certain times of the month.)

But Kimura claims that low oestrogen levels cause women to perform poorly on complex physical tasks requiring good co-ordination, including some tasks involving speech. In contrast, when oestrogen levels are high – briefly, just before ovulation, and again in the the last seven to ten days before menstruation – women do better at verbal tasks and those requiring precise physical movements, but have difficulty with spatial relations.

These results are puzzling. Few women have complained of finding it difficult to speak when they have their periods, or of finding it difficult to locate their cars when they are not menstruating. Throughout this work, the changes being talked about are, as Kimura acknowledges, 'quite small' – a few per cent difference on the average score of a group of women. In the verbal fluency test, women were asked to recite five times, without errors, 'A box of mixed biscuits in a biscuit mixer'. Women at their peak oestrogen levels cut three seconds off their average seventeen second time. According to Anne Fausto-Sterling, a biologist at Brown University, Rhode Island, these studies are flawed because 'the women knew why they were being tested and the testers knew what phase of the menstrual cycle the subjects were in' – making the results distinctly vulnerable to bias.[20]

Kimura admits that she has failed to discover any phase of the menstrual cycle that is characterised by 'either a generalised decrement or a generalised facilitation in women's performance'. In other words, there is no time of the month when women are rendered incompetent and incapable by their hormones. 'If anything,' Kimura surmises, 'the picture is one of complex minor trade-offs among different abilities.' What is more, 'the fact that the effects vary considerably in direction and degree among individual women emphasises the inappropriateness of judging any particular woman on the basis of these group results'. She points out that many studies have failed to detect any variations during the menstrual cycle in women's abilities to perform complex, real-life, intellectual tasks, such as university examinations. This suggests, contends Kimura, that 'one should not be too hasty in generalising these laboratory findings to everyday life'.

Yet Kimura also maintains that 'theoretically, these findings are very important'.[21] Why? Because they 'support the idea that male–female differences in cognitive patterns in humans are originally organized – and are still mediated by – sex hormones'. And this theory (discussed in detail in Chapter 4), appeals to psychobiologists such as Kimura because it claims that there is a fixed biological foundation for differences in the way women and men behave. The appeal of such foundational ideas, in turn, is very much part of the hidden politics of this research.

The Pathology of the Menses

'When you get political ferment about the changing roles of women,' argues Barbara Sommer, a psychologist at the University of California at Davis, 'that's when you find menstrual cycle research.'[22] In the earlier wave of feminism, at the turn of the century, a pioneering experimental psychologist, Leta Hollingworth, carried out some of the earliest research on the menstrual cycle. She found no evidence that access to higher education – then a contentious issue – damaged a woman's cycle, nor any sign that a woman's intellectual ability lessened at any particular point in the cycle.

The idea that a woman's menses are peculiarly vulnerable to pathology has a long history, but it was the Victorians who were especially obsessed with menstrual bleeding. Medical opinion urged that any mental effort on the part of women risked interrupting their menstrual flow. Menstruation was seen as an outward sign of sexual heat; a stoppage would represent the damming up of sexuality, a pollution that could end in insanity or even death.

Medical encyclopaedias produced for home consumption contained impressive lists of diseases of menstruation. John Forbes's 1833 *Cyclopaedia of Practical Medicine* has separate articles on amenorrhoea (retention and suppression of the menses), dysmenorrhoea (acute pain during menstruation), menorrhagia (morbidly profuse menstruation), the pathology of menstruation, and leucorrhoea (white vaginal discharge), as well as discussions of chlorosis, pregnancy, hysteria and puerperal diseases. As Sally Shuttleworth of the University of Leeds recounts:[23]

> To read through the entries is to gain an impression of a near-hysterical male anxiety focused on the flow of female secretions, and in particular those of menstruation – a hysteria whose impact on the female psyche must inevitably have been to create the sense of existing in an almost permanent state of pathology.

The clinicians of the day advocated treating women with no periods or 'half periods' by applications of electricity or galvanism to the pelvis; or by applying leeches once a month to the groin, labia, uterus or feet; or by surgically lancing the cervix and uterus. Such was the fear of obstruction that one medical paper stressed that 'the period ought not to pass over without detracting some blood, either from the uterus or its immediate neighbourhood'. Not surprisingly, the popular press regularly ran advertisements for various 'quack' medicines – 'female corrective pills' – which promised to ensure that menstrual flows would meet 'performance' criteria, and so forestall medical intervention. Women must sometimes have taken such medicines hoping to induce an abortion, but this was by no means their only selling point.

Where did this obsession with the uterine economy come from? Shuttleworth sees many links between the medical preoccupation with women's menstruation and contemporary social and cultural concerns. For instance, the fears of

45

obstruction and accumulated waste that dominated Victorian theories of female economy were also very relevant to the *laissez-faire* economics elaborated by economists such as Herbert Spencer. Like the body, the economy could thrive only with the free flow and circulation of commodities, unimpeded by blockage or government interference. But why the sudden concern about an uncontrollable outburst of female sexuality? A strong impetus behind Victorian ideologies of womanhood, Shuttleworth suggests, comes not from the need to control women, but 'rather from the problems involved in assimilating *men* to the new conditions of the labour market'.

The increasing social division of labour highlighted the question of sexual difference, while increasing industrialisation brought the disciplining of the labour force to the fore. Viewing the new industrial workplace, apologist and critic alike spoke of man as machine. But the idea of the worker as a mere cog within the larger machine was at odds with the celebration of man as rational, independent actor in the marketplace, celebrated in *laissez-faire* economics. Shuttleworth suggests that the Victorian ideologies of gender provided a way out of this contradiction; that the ideologies functioned 'as a displaced form of resolution':

Notions of gender differentiation fulfilled the ideological role of allowing the male sex to renew their faith in personal autonomy and control. Unlike women, men were not prey to the forces of the body, the unsteady oscillations of which mirrored the uncertain flux of social circulation; rather they were their own masters – not automatons or mindless parts of the social machinery but self-willed individuals, living incarnations of the rational individualists and self-made men of economic theory. The disruptive social forces that had to be so decisively channelled and regulated to ensure mastery and controlled circulation in the economic sphere were metronymically represented, however, in the domestic realm, in the internal bodily processes of the woman in the home.[24]

So women's physiology was conceptualised in a way that

resolved some of the conflicts inherent in men's experience of Victorian industrial capitalism. For women, this ideological solution could only have compounded their sense of inherent pathology. Women were advised to stay calm and cheerful during their menses: any anger, fear, grief or intellectual exertion would threaten menstruation, as 'every part of the animal economy is influenced by the passions, but none more so than this'. According to Shuttleworth: 'female thought and passion, like government intervention in the Spencerian model of the economy, created blockages and interference, throwing the whole organism into a state of disease'.

Is Premenstrual Syndrome a Disease?

Today women remain figures of radical instability, reflecting in part perceptions of a perilous economy that echo Victorian ones. In the twentieth century, scientists and doctors have continued to diagnose women and their premenstrual bodily changes as pathological, now generally in hormonal terms. But in the latest development, the American Psychiatric Association proposes to make premenstrual syndrome a recognised psychiatric disorder – 'late luteal phase dysphoric disorder'.[25]

Mari Rodin, a social scientist in La Jolla, California, draws another parallel with Victorian times – that famous female malaise known as hysteria.[26] This widespread and debilitating 'nervous' disorder was traced to the state of a woman's reproductive system and her failure properly to fulfil her role in society as wife and mother. Rodin argues that the alacrity with which the medical profession has adopted premenstrual syndrome as a legitimate disease category (applying for research funds, treating patients, opening PMS clinics), despite the fact that no one agrees on how to define it, what the symptoms are, and how to treat it, suggests that it is not so much scientific fact but 'shared cultural knowledge' that informs understandings of what constitutes premenstrual syndrome. In other words, women are expected to be liable to 'nervous disorders' and 'negative mood'.

Scientific research reinforces the stereotype, Rodin points out, through standardised questionnaires used to tap women's menstrual experience. The most popular research tool, the Moos Menstrual Distress Questionnaire, focuses on negative mood and behavioural changes. 'Consequently, any premenstrual experience that is at variance from the one offered by the questionnaire is impossible to detect.' This, she says, is how the researchers' concept of premenstrual syndrome is reaffirmed and reproduced. The alternative 'diary' approach, in which the woman notes her symptoms each day, is similarly slanted – most options available on the calendar are negative: 'Women's reports of their menstrual experience become reproductions of the medical description of PMS.'

Scientists hope to find the 'true' origins of the syndrome in terms of bodily processes that operate unsullied by any other influences. But the issue will not be resolved by physiological findings alone. As Rodin argues, 'the shared cultural knowledge penetrates into all of its aspects'. The diagnostic category PMS embodies a set of ideas about women, their reproductive system, and 'irrational' behaviour which are deeply rooted in Western culture. 'What needs to be acknowledged', argues Jacquelyn Zita of the University of Minnesota, 'is that our experience of the body is very likely symbolically mediated by ideologies and socio-cognitive factors that impact on how one interprets bodily states.'[27]

The concept of premenstrual syndrome remains a double-edged sword for women, as the American anthropologist Alma Gottlieb has argued.[28] Because it is attributed to hormones, it can be used, 'however unconsciously', as a vehicle for women to express legitimate discontent with the 'enervating machine of the daily domestic grind' without betraying their 'feminine allure'. But if premenstrual syndrome is used in this way, women's legitimate complaints remain unaddressed. Emily Martin, professor of anthropology at Johns Hopkins University, asks whether another view of premenstrual syndrome might not give women 'greater intrinsic dignity and worth'.[29]

Martin notes that many accounts of PMS focus on a loss of ability to carry on activities involving mental or physical discipline – described as difficulty in concentrating, forgetfulness, impaired judgement, lack of co-ordination and decreased efficiency. These are not dreadful symptoms, wholly negative whatever the circumstances, especially as they often seem to go hand in hand with increased capacities and beneficial consequences. For instance, many women, Martin argues, report a sense of enhanced emotional responsiveness, creativity or sensuality which they find valuable and rewarding. But the symptoms of loss that are the usual focus of attention remain unfortunate in the particular social and economic system we live in, with the kind of work it generates. In short, the symptoms reveal an 'intolerance for the kind of work discipline required by late industrial societies'.

Similarly, accounts of premenstrual anger assume that it threatens to disrupt social relations within the family, and that it is the woman's responsibility to seek medical help to control it: 'What is missing is any consideration of why, in Western societies, women might feel extreme rage at a time when their usual emotional controls are reduced.'

Anthropologists have long agreed that spirit possession in traditional societies is often a means by which politically weak individuals – usually women – express discontent and manipulate their superiors. But in these societies the possession, and the social response to it, bring a community together over some dispute and put social relationships to rights. 'In our own inverted version of these elements,' writes Martin, 'women say they feel "possessed" but what the society sees as behind their trouble is really their own malfunctioning bodies.' The result is that 'attention is necessarily shunted away from the social environment in which the "possession" arose'. In our culture, the woman's anger is not seen as really her fault, but neither is it to be taken seriously. Martin suggests that this diffuse anger could spring from women's perception, however inarticulate, of their oppression in society: 'of their lowered wage scales, lesser opportunities for advancement into high ranks, tacit omission from the language, coercion into roles, inside the family and out, that demand constant nurturance and self denial – to only begin the list'.

By 1993, the backlash against the idea of premenstrual syndrome was well under way. At a spring meeting of the British

Psychological Society, several researchers presented results that cast doubt on the existence of PMS, picked up by the newspapers with headlines such as 'PMS may be all in the mind' and 'Time of the month? A thing of the past'.[30] By the summer, women's magazines began to feature articles with pictures of sultry-looking women headlined: 'This Woman is Premenstrual (So How Come She Feels So Good?)', 'The PMS Myth', and 'Surprise! The Good News About PMS – 25% of women say they feel better before their periods'.[31]

This positive reporting did not necessarily mean that hormonal determinism had been entirely jettisoned. Readers of *Company* were advised to indulge their carbohydrate cravings with equanimity because it would rectify the brain chemical imbalance supposedly brought about by their monthly 'hormonal surges'. *New Woman* reported that women could feel better and sexier premenstrually because their testosterone levels were elevated. But the magazine's reporter, Lisa Sussman, went on to argue that the symptomatology for PMS was so vague and all-encompassing that it included 'every feeling and problem under the sun. At this rate, who wouldn't have PMS?'

The centrepiece of the *New Woman* story, echoed in the editor's leader, was an unattributed study of men. They were given a checklist of symptoms, such as headaches, food cravings, fatigue and job anxiety, and asked to tick the ones they had experienced in the past month. Most of the men had experienced many of these symptoms. But when they were given the same list, this time entitled 'Menstrual Distress Questionnaire', these same symptoms mysteriously disappeared. 'The men may have similar symptoms,' Sussman writes, 'but they don't have a label for it.'

Sussman concludes that the 'PMS myth' persists because drug companies can sell their cures, men can keep telling PMS jokes against their female work colleagues, and at a pinch, a woman can fall back on it as an excuse 'when letting loose with socially unacceptable unfeminine behaviour – like anger, ambition or aggression'. 'Don't forget,' she concludes: 'Real equality means never having to say you're premenstrual.'

50

The debate continues. *The Observer* fought back with the saga of one woman's story of severe PMS, and Katharina Dalton's treatment of her, under the headline, 'Why women are angry every month'.[32]

Biorhythms for Men

The founding fathers of the science of hormones viewed the body as striving for a 'steady state' or 'equilibrium'. Hormones were seen as helping to achieve the constancy of the 'internal milieu'. It is now clear that the hormone levels of everyone – not just women – are changing all the time. Yet they become the focus of interest and concern only when they are regarded as having gone awry in individuals who fail to keep step with the world. Unable to find straightforward abnormalities in hormone levels at any one moment, researchers have begun to look for hidden pathologies in an individual's 'time structure'.

Several hormones show a more or less regular pattern of rise and fall over a twenty-four-hour period.[33] Such cycles are known as circadian rhythms, from the Latin *circa diem*, 'about a day'. Cortisol, from the adrenal gland, usually peaks at between 6 and 8 a.m., while adrenaline peaks in the afternoon. These rhythms are largely independent of sleep and wakefulness, and carry on regardless of what a person does. Body temperature, sleepiness and levels of a hormone called melatonin also tend to persist in their rhythm whatever a person's circumstances.

But these cycles eventually drift out of phase if a person is isolated from the outside world and prevented from carrying out their normal routine. Biologists argue that one or more inner 'clocks' drive these roughly twenty-four-hour cycles, but that the clock needs to be set to the correct time by something in the environment. Without such synchronisers, various cycles can drift apart or become generally flattened or dampened down. Light is the most obvious of these time-checks, or *Zeitgebers*, and the one most frequently studied.

One of the most intriguing things about these well-established circadian rhythms is that they have no obvious role in life. No one knows why, for instance, the hormone that controls the thyroid gland, the so-called thyroid stimulating hormone, should rise in the evening and decline during sleep. Prolactin is one of the few hormones apparently released directly in response to sleep, again for no known reason. Levels rise steeply after a person has fallen asleep, and reach a peak about three hours later, but not if sleep is prevented. Prolactin does all sorts of things at other times – it enhances milk production in nursing mothers, conserves water in the kidneys, helps to control electrolyte levels, and perhaps influences the metabolism of glucose and fats. What it is doing in sleep is still a mystery.

Growth hormone is perhaps the only cyclical hormone that has a vaguely plausible theory to go with it. Growth hormone floods into the bloodstream during the first three hours of sleep, reaching its peak in the period of deep sleep known as slow-wave sleep. None is released if a person stays awake. Jim Horne, a sleep researcher at Loughborough University, argues that the surge of growth hormone during sleep may be the body's way of coping with the overnight fast: the hormone may encourage the body to use fat instead of valuable protein as an energy source.[34] It also stimulates growth in children – so perhaps children grow only in their sleep. Growth hormone also seems to have a mild stimulating effect on the immune system, at least in laboratory rats; this could help to explain why sleep is good for you. But all these ideas remain speculative.

Hormone of Darkness

The most mysterious of all hormonal cycles is that of melatonin.[35] This hormone has a pronounced daily rhythm: it is light, or the lack of it, that determines how much is produced. Melatonin is made in the pineal gland, a tiny, pine-cone-shaped structure buried deep in the brain. A tortuous pathway of nerves connects the light-sensitive retina of the eye to the pineal. Thanks to this connection, the gland releases melatonin only in darkness; daylight inhibits its release. The circadian rhythm in this hormone thus mostly depends on the shifting hours of dark and light, regardless of sleep or wakefulness. Normal indoor lighting at night, and moonlight, are too dim to suppress its release, but very bright light at night – intensities of 2500 lux or more, about four or five times the intensity of normal room lighting – can decrease concentrations in the blood. On the other hand, being in the dark for a while during the day – going to see a film, say – does not increase melatonin secretion. Blind people whose retinas are insensitive to light still have melatonin cycles of about 24.7 hours – but the highest values can be in either the day or the night.

The precise function of melatonin remains obscure. In some seasonally breeding mammals, such as deer or wallabies, it seems to form part of an inbuilt calendar that works by sensing the changing daylength. Melatonin helps to prime the reproductive system for the arrival of spring (or whenever the breeding season is). It can also influence growth in some young mammals, again on a seasonal basis – hastening growth when food is plentiful and slowing it during the winter.

Many researchers believe that in humans the hormone is tied up with an inner clock that generates rhythms in body temperature and cortisol, secreted by the outer layer of the adrenal glands. Researchers studying shift workers or jet-setters have discovered that during and immediately after a change to night-shift work or travel across time zones, the secretion of melatonin depends more on the clock than on the light–dark cycle. It seems plausible to suppose that this temporary desynchronisation may contribute to jet lag, and that melatonin might reset the clock. As a result, melatonin has been much vaunted as a treatment for sufferers from jet lag. In one study, volunteers taking melatonin after a flight from San Francisco to London did report fewer symptoms than those taking a placebo. But the beneficial effects of taking a dose at bedtime might just be due to the sleep, the researchers concluded, for melatonin is a mild sleep-inducer.

It is not even a very convincing sleeping draught, as mammals that are active in the night secrete it too. The hormone might promote sleep by some circuitous route, acting as a modulator of putative sleep-inducing substances in the brain, but there is no evidence for this. Melatonin levels also decline with age; this might have something to do with changing qualities of sleep. One researcher, Russel Reiter of the University of Texas at San Antonio, thinks that melatonin prevents ageing, and speculates that melatonin supplements may turn out to be 'the fountain of youth'.[36] But his reasoning is largely circumstantial, and few scientists have yet been convinced by his arguments.

Melatonin has also been implicated in various mental illnesses, especially depression, but again not very convincingly. Several studies have found no difference in the melatonin secretion of depressed patients. Some researchers have pointed to the fact that the incidence of depression peaks in the spring, with a smaller peak in the autumn, and suggested that this peaking is due to the rapid change in the length of day at these times. The idea is that the synchronisation of circadian rhythms by the light–dark cycle becomes rather problematic around the equinoxes. But no one has found consistent changes in melatonin levels that would support this theory, according to one melatonin specialist, Josephine Arendt of the University of Surrey.[37]

Nonetheless, it is widely believed that melatonin plays a key role in an unusual form of depression known as seasonal affective disorder. People diagnosed as suffering from this syndrome suddenly become depressed in the autumn, crave carbohydrates and put on weight, only to recover their spirits and shed their extra pounds in the spring. Research groups have treated sufferers by having them stare into very bright lights for several hours each morning or evening, to mimic the light conditions of a long summer's day. Others question whether this syndrome really exists, and point to the likelihood of a strong placebo effect.

The importance of light in unaffected individuals is still unknown. Depressed individuals prescribed light therapy are exposed to lights of an intensity of 2500 lux. Outdoor workers see up to 100,000 lux on a sunny day, while office workers in winter rarely see more than 1000 lux. If light levels were crucial to normal functioning, why aren't all those office workers ill?

Mentally Ill Because 'Out of Sync'?

It has become fashionable recently to link various other psychiatric ills – especially schizophrenia and severe depression – to some internal desynchronisation of body rhythms. A popular theory is that there are two central rhythm-generating systems which become out of step in the mentally ill, resulting in periodic clinical symptoms.[38] Different studies have reported low melatonin levels and high cortisol levels in depressed or schizophrenic patients, but the evidence continues to be poor. 'It remains debatable whether good internal synchronisation of rhythms is important for well-being or not,' Arendt concludes.[39] She points out that it is just as likely that psychological unhappiness leads to desynchronisation. Disrupted sleep patterns might eventually lead to the suppression of melatonin levels, for instance. A small percentage of apparently normal men have no detectable melatonin rhythm – suggesting that the pineal gland does not do anything of major importance, at least in adult men.

With this focus on internal rhythms, the importance of the individual's social world becomes obscured. Much of our knowledge of circadian rhythms comes from isolation experiments where people are locked away from as much of the outside world as possible to live shielded from any time cues, even putative *Zeitgebers* from outer space. A young Italian woman, who broke the world record for time spent isolated in an underground cave, became so depressed that she lost a fifth of her body weight while she was underground. In 1990 another woman, who broke the Italian's world record, committed suicide in Los Angeles, a year after she emerged from isolation. A psychiatrist who interviewed her said she was depressed when she left the cave. In both these cases, depression may have stemmed from the loss of synchronisers from the outside world, leading to the desynchronisation of biological cycles. Being in low light might have altered melatonin levels. But loneliness and the interruption of habitual social support must remain strong contenders as the ultimate sources of their despair.[40]

Social support and stimulation, or the lack of it, may also

account for some of the hormonal aberrations sometimes reported among the mentally ill, not least via an effect on the quality of sleep. Horne has suggested that high-quality slow-wave sleep seems to be inordinately influenced by the extent to which a person has engaged with their surroundings during the day. In his experiments with volunteers living in a university's sleep laboratory, a day out sightseeing was followed by a marked increase in slow-wave sleep at night.

This sort of deep sleep is often virtually absent in people with schizophrenia or severe depression, Horne reports. Perhaps people with these disorders lose interest in the outside world and are preoccupied with their own thoughts. Slow-wave sleep also coincides with the release of growth hormone, tenuously linked with positive changes in the immune system. 'Here may be another link between psychological well-being and the effectiveness of the immune response to ward off infection,' suggests Horne. Increased interest in and awareness of one's surroundings might lead to more slow-wave sleep, and a greater night-time boost to the immune system. If daytime life is overly stressful, cortisol levels will rise, so suppressing the immune response. But loss of interest in one's daily life over the long term, as in depression, could suppress deep sleep and increase vulnerability to disease. Such ideas are speculative, but they give a flavour of some of the ways in which social life and sense of well-being may be profoundly enmeshed with 'the body'.

Meanwhile, the physiologists' hope of finding a clock ticking away somewhere in the human brain – the favourite contender today is the suprachiasmatic nucleus of the hypothalamus – is no closer to fulfilment. Single-celled creatures have rhythms too, making them ideal subjects for laboratory chronobiologists. Yet no one has yet tracked down the ticking molecules. In the primitive organism *Acetabularia* – a one-celled marine green algae – both the cell's genetic centre, the nucleus, and the surrounding material, the cytoplasm, can maintain periodicities in behaviour even in the face of drugs that stop the synthesis of the key genetic messenger, RNA. There seems to be more than one oscillator producing independent rhythms, creating mind-boggling complexity, even in a single cell. And these organisms remain interconnected and sensitive to information provided by the environment. 'One must note that the search for the elusive clock per se could be doomed to failure if circadian timekeeping is not attributable to any one entity or subset of reactions in a cell,' concludes one contemporary researcher in the field.[41] He ruefully quotes a colleague's comment, published sixteen years ago: 'The clock, volatile as a ghost, lurks now in one room, now in another.' Virtually every aspect of cell chemistry seems to be involved in biological rhythms.

Compared to the study of cancer, genetics, even gynaecology, chronobiology remains a poorly funded and ill-defined speciality within the biomedical sciences. The discovery that drugs can have very different effects depending on when you take them has inspired some recent interest in 'chronopharmacology'. Clinical laboratory specialists have also noted that the complexity of the 'multifrequency human time structure' rather complicates the task of interpreting the analysis of blood and urine samples. But neither of these findings has really made much impact on everyday clinical practice.

Clocks for the Boys

One strategy to make cyclicity seem more acceptable as a concept to be applied to men, and thereby boost the status of chronobiology as a speciality, is to associate the research with that quintessentially masculine pursuit, sport. This approach is being pursued by a team of researchers at the NASA/Ames Research Center in California.[42] 'If a soccer coach wants his team to execute several new and exciting plays for next week's championship game, the science of chronobiology suggests that the best time to introduce the plays is 3 in the afternoon,' the NASA researchers confidently predict. They claim to be able to foretell when a person's 'physiological mechanisms' should function optimally – with 'implications for space flight, agriculture, military training, teaching, business, medicine, psychiatry and other fields besides competitive athletics' which require peak mental and physical performance. Any deviation from the optimal circadian 'window' can lead to significant decrements in peak performance. Reserve for the morning activities dependent on short-term memory, and devote the afternoon to anything requiring long-term memory, the researchers advise. Shotputters should aim to throw at 1700 hours, while swimmers should wait till 2200.

While such detailed advice does indeed link cyclicity with masculine strength and triumphal achievement rather than focusing, as is typical of women's cycles, on the supposedly 'bad' phases, these chronobiologists risk overplaying their hand. By claiming so much for the predictive powers of their science, they risk a backlash from more conservative colleagues in other fields, and chronobiology's relegation to the backwaters as a cranky, eccentric pursuit at best, at worst a pseudo-science.

But chronobiology is being genderised to its advantage through another route – by calling on what is seen as perhaps the most rigorous and prestigious sciences of them all: the study of the structure and function of the human brain. Neuroanatomists claim to have found a difference between male and female human brains in the region believed to contain the elusive 'master clock'.

Several years ago, Dick Swaab and his colleague M.A. Hofman at the Netherlands Institute for Brain Research in Amsterdam, began investigating a tiny region known as the superchiasmatic nucleus (SCN). This cluster of cells in the hypothalamus of the brain is believed to control circadian rhythms such as sleep–wake cycles, although no one yet knows how it might do so. This nucleus intrigued Swaab and Hofman, however, because it also seemed to be involved in other rhythmic phenomena, notably the menstrual cycle, making the structure 'of special interest for the study of sex differences'. By staining and slicing several human brains and counting cells under the microscope, the Dutch researchers made a startling discovery: although the overall volume, cell density, and total number of cells in the SCN turned out to be virtually identical in both sexes, there appears to be a difference in its shape. A woman's superchiasmatic nucleus tends to be slightly longer and thinner than the shorter, fatter ones possessed by men. Swaab and Hofman claim that their discovery is the first clear demonstration of a sex difference in human brain cells, although 'the functional implication of the SCN shape difference is still obscure'.[43]

For Swaab and Hofman, what is significant is the finding of neuroanatomical difference between men and women. Twice, in a paper published in 1984, they refer to Germaine Greer as the supposedly dogmatic feminist denying the scientific evidence that male and female brains function differently, when in fact Greer is pointing to the political interpretations loaded on to reports of difference. What the brain researchers do not seem to appreciate is that in this context difference is inexorably political – or, indeed, that their work is considered interesting and important only because of our shared cultural concerns with the roots of gender. No one has any idea what functional significance a minute difference in shape might have, but even that is beside the point. Difference is to be expected: women menstruate; men do not. What is at issue is the origin and significance of this difference, and these are culturally loaded questions. It is rather like a scientist announcing that men who lift weights have larger muscles than men who don't, and then implying that this difference tells us something interesting about the intrinsic nature of different types of people. Feminists do not deny difference; they question scientific explanations of its sources and its significance in our lives.

3

HORMONAL HAVOC

APPETITE, STRESS AND AGGRESSION

A spate of films – *Alien* and its sequels, werewolf films such as *The Howling*, David Cronenberg's remake of *The Fly* – turn on the eruption from within the body of some alien, libidinous, uncontrollable entity. In *Alien* the creature emerges from an egg, attaches itself to a crew member's face, and deposits its seed deep within his body. There it gestates, until it finally bursts out of the man's stomach in a particularly gruesome scene much admired by aficionados of special effects. But the enduring horror of the film lies in the image of our harbouring the 'other' within – in the notion that within our bodies lies something alien that can burst out of control, with lethal effects. Why do these images have such currency for us today?

They are symptomatic, argues Susan Bordo, of deep psycho-cultural anxieties surrounding the control of the body, especially its desires and impulses.[1] Our preoccupation with the 'internal' management of the body represents dis-placed fears and tensions stemming from instabilities in the social and economic spheres. We use images of the body symbolically to reproduce the central vulnerabilities and anxieties of the larger world, the 'social body'.

Bordo elaborates this interpretation by exploring current preoccupations with food and slender bodies, as evinced in the phenomenon of eating disorders. But similar concerns, I argue, also underlie contemporary approaches to stress and its management, as well as attitudes towards and interpretations of male violence. In each case, hormones form part of the social and medical construction of inner processes seen to be in need of control. Ideas about hormones also function as powerful normalising strategies. They help to foster the production of self-monitoring and self-disciplining 'docile bodies', sensitive to departures from social norms, and habituated to self-improvement.

Fatness, Thinness and the Social Body

A generation ago, the average fashion model weighed 8 per cent less than the average woman; now, models are 23 per cent lighter. Girls who play with Barbie dolls receive a similar message: the world's bestselling doll is so thin that, were she human, she would be anorectic. Since 1960, the winners of the Miss America pageant and the women portrayed in *Playboy*'s nude centrefold have become progressively thinner. The latest goal is a 'firmer toned', muscular body, created by the woman who eats little but 'works out' to banish fat and flab.[2]

This cultural valorisation of thinness is widely cited as a cause of eating disorders, and women's widespread concern about food. Sociologists and cultural commentators increasingly see eating disorders as extreme symptoms of social pressures on women in general. Low self-esteem, rigid dieting and negative body image are experienced by perhaps the majority of women today, as the historical shift towards feminine thinness and self-restraint continues to intensify.[3]

But there are other, less obvious, forces at work. In the consumer cultures of the West, Bordo argues, the body demonstrates the 'correct' management of desire. Fatness is feared and loathed because it is 'a metaphor for anxiety about internal processes out of control – uncontained desire, un-restrained hunger, uncontrolled impulse'. Why is desire per-ceived as being so difficult to control? Bordo finds the answer in a consumer culture that forces individuals to develop a contradictory double-bind personality, reflecting the contra-dictions of the economy at large. As 'producer-selves', indi-viduals must control their desires for immediate gratification and cultivate the work ethic. But as 'consumer-selves', 'we serve the system through a boundless capacity to capitulate to desire and indulge in impulse; we must become creatures who hunger for constant and immediate satisfaction'. So, in her view, the regulation of desire becomes an ongoing problem, 'as we find ourselves continually besieged by temptation while socially condemned for overindulgence'.

Food and diet become the central arenas for the expression of these contradictions. In a culture of overabundance built on ever-increasing consumption of material goods, individuals are pressured in gendered ways to manage their desire, to develop the correct 'attitude': a slim, well-muscled body now suggests 'willpower, energy, control over infantile impulse, the ability to "make something" of oneself'. Bordo argues that the pressures on women are particularly severe. In patri-archal societies, the management of female desire is seen as especially difficult; women's desires are regarded as 'other', mysterious, threatening to destroy the established order. Hunger and appetite become a code for female desire; a slen-der, androgynous body is a route to containment. Yet such a body image can have a very different meaning: it can also symbolise 'the liberation of female desire from a domestic, reproductive destiny'. The fact that the slender female body can carry both these (seemingly contradictory) meanings is one reason 'for its compelling attraction in periods of gender change'. Dieting came into its own during the 1920s, as women finally won the right to vote. Twiggy appeared in *Vogue* in 1965, as the contraceptive Pill launched the 'sexual revolution'.

The Psychiatrists' Account

The clinical presentation of anorexia and bulimia underlines the suggestion that something peculiar is going on in our culture. Anorexia most often strikes adolescents between the ages of fourteen and eighteen, although it is now said to be becoming more common among younger children. Almost all sufferers (probably 95 per cent) are female. Anorexia usually begins with a diet, something which most contemporary adolescent girls attempt at some time. But for the potential anorectic, dieting begins to yield a powerful sense of control. And in a society that puts a premium on thinness, losing weight is a special triumph.[4]

The most recent development has been the surge of cases of a new pattern, binge eating and vomiting in individuals who maintain a normal weight. The syndrome, bulimia nervosa, was first described in detail by Gerald Russell of the Institute of Psychiatry in London in 1979, and is now considered to be more common than anorexia.

Susie Orbach, a psychotherapist and author of *Hunger Strike*, finds the roots of these conditions in an individual's psychological development in specific social and cultural contexts.[5] Like Bordo, she emphasises the problematic nature of desire, especially for girls and women. Girls brought up in the West today are schooled to tend to the needs of others, first and foremost, and often come to see their own needs as somehow illegitimate. For some women, refusing food then becomes a way of controlling desire. The body, as a source of illegitimate needs and desires, is experienced as an alien object that must be controlled, or it will take control. Anorectic women speak of the twin fears of gaining weight and 'going out of control'. Starving the body establishes the individual's triumph over it, and over the unpredictable appearance of need. All this happens in a cultural context in which female bodies are constantly represented as objects, and ever thinner objects at that, so reinforcing the anorectic's alienation.

Bulimics, too, experience their bodies as disconnected from their selves, and diet to gain control. For them, binges of overeating represent a terrifying outburst of desire, a temporary loss of control. The official psychiatric description of bulimia stresses the patients' 'impulsive behaviour'.

Meanwhile, biomedical researchers have sought an inner cause for eating disorders: a biological factor that might lie at the root of anorexia or bulimia, and could provide the knowledge needed to devise a means of 'managing' sufferers' bodies. The researchers argue that disruptions to normal eating patterns have all sorts of consequences for bodily mechanisms. Reduce the amount of food you eat for several days, and levels of growth hormone fall. Drop 20 per cent below the norm in body weight, and the neuro-endocrinal link-ups that control menstruation pack in, causing the body to revert to a prepubertal state. Fasting also seems to disrupt brain neurotransmitters, as the supply of the precursors for these brain messengers dries up. Some of these changes may alter sensations of hunger and satiety, so perpetuating the avoidance of food and creating an illness that helps to feed itself.

But despite all their endeavours, researchers have yet to pinpoint the alien within – the deviant chemical that brings on the disease, or even fosters it once it is in place. Virtually all these abnormalities return to normal when eating begins again and weight is regained. The biological factors look like consequences of starvation, not causes. As Paul Garfinkel, an influential Canadian psychiatrist at the Clarke Institute of Psychiatry in Toronto, concludes: 'it is unlikely that either anorexia or bulimia will be cured by a single pharmacologic agent'.[6] Yet the search for an effective cocktail of drugs continues.

Fatness: Desire Run Rampant?

Fatness has, if anything, inspired even more research than excessive thinness. Adipose tissue has come to symbolise all that is most abhorred in Western capitalist cultures. It is as if fatness, especially in women, represents the ultimate failure to be a good citizen – to practise, somehow, both consumption and self-control. In cultural metaphor, as Bordo argues, it represents the capitulation to consumerism, the ultimate failure of self-control.

Influenced by this ideological baggage, the biomedical research community has searched long and hard for the 'defect' in those who are deemed overweight. Much of the research to date has looked for hormonal differences that could explain why people possess different amounts of body fat. Many people, lay and expert alike, remain convinced that if fatness is not a sin, it must be a disease. They hope to discover a chemical abnormality – something, perhaps a hormone, that causes some individuals to eat more than they metabolise. The cure might then lie in a drug that corrects the defect.

Without a doubt, food has powerful effects on our bodies – in many ways, it is the strongest drug around. The mere taste of sweetness can release a wave of the neurotransmitter dopamine in a putative 'reward' centre of the brain. Foods set up a cascade of biochemical events in the unconscious autonomic nervous system, and stimulate the release of hormones in the gut, even before they have begun to be digested and absorbed into the bloodstream. Once absorbed, the digested components of food profoundly modify the biochemistry of virtually all of the body, even the brain.

Given this bewildering array of events linked to the consumption of food, few physiologists expect a simple explanation. Our eating habits are taken to be the result of complex controls operating at different levels within the body. The complexity is said to explain why no one has yet found the answer. Belief remains strong, however, that we need only open the 'black box' and study the mechanisms inside in order to understand why some people become obese while others starve themselves.

Medical researchers have sought signs of a hormonal defect in the obese, but without success. The average metabolic rate of fat and lean individuals is generally comparable, and fat individuals are no more likely than thin ones to produce abnormally low levels of thyroid hormone. Drugs that could safely increase metabolic rate remain the dieter's great hope, but so far, nothing on the market quite fits the bill. The thyroid hormone thyroxine does indeed increase resting metabolic rate, and was once commonly prescribed – particularly in North America – for individuals trying to lose weight. Once again, the medical profession regarded hormones as a bit of internal machinery that they could alter without untoward consequences. But thyroid supplements are now frowned upon as a dieting aid for people with normal thyroid glands. Taking the hormone as a drug suppresses the body's own natural production. At the dosages required to achieve significant weight loss, dangerous side-effects, such as altered heart function, are common, and the hormone promotes the loss of muscle rather than fat. Lower doses can prevent the fall in metabolic rate that goes along with low-energy diets, but even then, muscle protein is lost at an alarming rate.

Other hormones can also boost metabolic rate – notably, adrenaline and noradrenaline. But they also cause the heart to beat more rapidly, perhaps leading to dangerous arrhythmias, and can cause anxiety, restlessness and insomnia. Researchers still hope to invent a drug that raises metabolic rate harmlessly.

In the attempt to find something that would suppress a person's desire to eat, doctors once prescribed amphetamine or 'speed' for their obese patients – until it became clear that it is not only addictive but can cause acute psychotic states similar to schizophrenia. The drug is a powerful stimulant of the central nervous system, and causes the release of noradrenaline. Modification of the amphetamine molecule has yielded other drugs that are less addictive but still reduce hunger, most notably fenfluramine. Unfortunately, these drugs also have unpleasant side-effects: sleeplessness, palpitations, dry mouth, nervousness and irritability or, in fenfluramine's case, drowsiness, diarrhoea and a tendency to depression if the drug is suddenly withdrawn.[7]

Appetising Hormones

In the pharmaceutical world, interest now centres on the quest to understand how appetite is normally dampened down after a meal. Various hormones produced by the gut in response to food – cholecystokinin, pancreatic glucagon and bombesin-like peptides, somatostatin and oxytocin – might just conceivably provide the clue to an effective anti-eating drug. Yet the sheer number of hormones that appear to be involved in one way or another is daunting. Eight other peptides (or small proteins) have also been potentially implicated in the control of satiety. Even the most committed hormonalists now agree that there is unlikely to be a simple answer to the riddle of appetite.

Several decades ago, many scientists were convinced that the brain held the key to hunger or repleteness. Animal experiments encouraged the idea that particular regions at the base of the brain act as feeding and satiety centres. But over the years the interpretation of these results has changed, and things now seem far less simple.[8] Interest has shifted to the array of signals from different parts of the body reaching the brain – with the hypothalamus as more of a telephone exchange than a command centre. The idea that the hypothalamus oversees food intake by signalling a 'set point' for body weight has become popular. But the set-point theory assumes that there is some way in which the brain can know what an individual's fat content is. So far, every attempt to find a metabolic signal that the brain could use to chart nutritional status and control food intake has failed. There is no sign of a 'master' signal – hormonal or otherwise – that would determine what, or when, or how much we eat.

Moreover, there seems to be no straightforward way of defining when an individual's eating behaviour has moved out of a 'regulated system or normal control'.[9] Most obese people eat in ways that are indistinguishable from those of normal-weight people, reports John Garrow, an obesity specialist in London: 'It is certain that if a videotape was made of every particle of food consumed by an assorted group of subjects it would be impossible for an independent observer to deduce from the eating pattern if the subject to which it referred was fat or thin.'[10]

Yet the belief in the existence – and the enlightened nature – of biological explanations persists. Two American psychiatrists, Albert Stunkard and Thomas Wadden, recently described a 'revolutionary' change in perspectives on human obesity. 'There has been a 180-degree change in direction in our views of causality during the past two decades,' they claim.[11] Experts used to think that obesity was caused by 'emotional disturbance' and 'failed impulse control'. Freudians claimed that obese people had an emotional disorder that caused them to overeat to relieve their anxiety and depression, which resulted from a libido fixated in the oral phase. The origins of obesity was thus thought to lie in 'profound psychological disturbances buried deep within the patient', Stunkard and Wadden write. If the treatment failed, the explanation similarly lay with the patient.

It is now apparent, these psychiatrists claim, that any anxiety and depression experienced by the seriously overweight are likely to be due to 'living in a society that derogates obesity and obese persons', and to the stresses of continual attempts to restrict food intake. Now, they conclude, the cause of the obesity is properly understood – thanks to 'the convincing biologic explanations' of the origins of obesity. Yet there is in fact no convincing biological account, no identifiable bodily trait, that can explain why some people become obese and others do not – nor do the psychiatrists suggest a candidate. It is just that they think there must be one.

Appetising Times

Explanations founded exclusively on internal mechanisms find it difficult to account for a phenomenon as rich and diverse as eating. A biological account cannot tell us why, in some cultures, fat is desirable – a sign of wealth and status – or why, in Euro-American cultures, thinness has become the ultimate object of desire. Taste in eating, and even appetite itself, have undergone a transformation since the Middle Ages, according to sociologist Stephen Mennell.[12] This history of the 'civilising of appetite' demonstrates, perhaps more strongly than any other evidence, that how much people eat is intimately intertwined with social, cultural and psychological influences.

Building on the work of the sociologist Norbert Elias, Mennell links this civilising process to broad changes in the structure of society in Europe since medieval times. In the Middle Ages the rich had much more to eat than the poor, but everyone had to live through periods of scarcity. There was a shift away from cycles of feasting and fasting, plenty and want, as the security of food supplies increased in early modern Europe – because of profound social changes in trading patterns, division of labour and the formation of secure nation-states.

The gargantuan blow-outs once characteristic of the rich began to give way to an emphasis on discrimination at table. By the late seventeenth and early eighteenth centuries, as more people were able to match the consumption of their social superiors, displays of vast quantities of food became vulgar, and elaborate and delicate concoctions became the fashion. At the same time, value began to be placed on internalised self-control rather than the ability to gorge oneself at a feast.

By the early 1700s the medical profession had begun to advocate restraint in appetite. Gradually, the physical bulk traditionally seen as a metaphor for moral weight and social *gravitas* became replaced by a preference for slenderness and spirituality, as reflected in the novels of the day, as Pat Rogers of the University of South Florida has explored. Rogers argues that in the eighteenth century slimming concerned men as much as women, and was regarded as a matter of health as much as body image.[13]

By the nineteenth century, bourgeois gastronomes stressed the virtues of moderation, and frowned on obesity, which had began to move down the social scale. But fear of fatness had not yet become universal: at the end of the century, books and articles aimed at the lower middle class still advised readers on how to become plump. By the twentieth century, however, the social standards of expected self-restraint had become applicable to everyone, and 'slimming' books and magazines began to flood the popular market. The social pressures, especially on women, to show self-restraint through an ever thinner body have continued to escalate. Today, most women in

Western culture – perhaps as many as 90 per cent – constantly monitor the amount they eat, and eat less than they need to stop them feeling hungry. What constitutes 'normal' eating for women today is decidedly not a matter of biology.[14]

Stressful Hormones: Who's In Control?

Ideas about stress also centre around notions of inner chemistry in need of control. The human need for empowerment – to feel in control of one's day-to-day life – is transposed on to the body, to appear once again as the duty to practise 'self-control'.

On the face of it, the science of stress seems straightforward. Stress, after all, is by definition a matter of hormones: scientists judge something to be stressful only if it stimulates the release of eponymous stress hormones. It turns out that almost anything can provoke a stress response. 'Stressors' range from physiological insults such as surgical incisions, exposure to electric shocks or temperatures that are too high or too low, to life events such as redundancy, unemployment, bereavement or divorce.[15]

These unpleasant experiences have virtually nothing in common, yet each triggers much the same constellation of hormonal responses. For instance, stressors always trigger the hormone adrenaline, as Walter Cannon, one of the fathers of stress physiology, discovered in the early years of this century. This hormone is produced by the core, or medulla, of the adrenal gland. Cannon termed this the 'fight or flight response'.[16]

Hans Selye, regarded as the co-founder of modern stress research, discovered the second archetypal stress hormone, cortisol.[17] Selye showed that stress also stimulates the adrenal's outer layer, its so-called cortex, to release hormones called glucocorticoids. Cortisol is the major representative of these in humans. Cortisol and adrenaline are responsible for the bulk of the effects attributed to stress, but scores of other hormones play a part. This hormonal whirlwind is beautifully designed to mobilise energy stores for emergency action and speed their delivery to heart, brain and muscle. Long-term bodily projects, such as building muscle or keeping gonads in reproductive order, are shut down, as is digestion. A body under stress is living for the moment in a big way. Even the immune system is suppressed, as is the perception of pain.

Selye first discovered the down side of the stress response by accident. Investigating the physiological effects of what he thought was a new hormone, he injected rats with extracts of ovarian tissue every day for several weeks. The rats developed stomach ulcers, abnormally large adrenal glands, and shrunken tissues of the immune system. He thought he had found a powerful new hormone – until he looked at the control rats, which had received injections of a harmless saline solution instead. They suffered identical symptoms. Selye concluded that it was the stress of the daily injections, not his putative hormone extract, that was to blame for the rats' condition. He tested his theory by stressing rats in other ways – subjecting them to cold, heat, extensive bleeding and illness. Every time the rats developed the same range of physical ills. The science of 'stress pathophysiology' was born.

It is now painfully clear that in experimental animals chronic and severe stress can lead to muscle wasting and fatigue, infertility, impotence, loss of libido, heart disease, ulcers, stunted growth and perhaps even cancer, as a result of the suppression of the immune system. Recent research suggests that chronic stress may also damage the hippocampus, a part of the brain intimately involved in memory and learning.

But there is more. The stress response turns out not to be cut and dried; it depends on an animal's perceptions and beliefs about the world, and ability to act effectively in it. A nasty experiment on animals makes the point. Deprive two monkeys of food, but give one something tasty yet calorie-free, such as flavoured water. The monkey with the flavoured water does not secrete cortisol, while the other one shows a marked stress response. Nothing in the explanatory world of the traditional stress physiologist could have predicted this outcome, because both monkeys remain, physiologically speaking, equally stressed. Both have equally depressed levels of blood glucose, for instance. The only difference is that the one fed the flavoured placebo perceives things differently – it thinks it has received a meal.

Hundreds of similar studies have highlighted the key elements of stress. These experiments have often been conducted at great cost to the animals concerned, and by recounting their findings here I do not wish to condone them. One general principle, however, has emerged from this work: what makes a stressful event really stressful is lack of control and lack of predictability.[18]

Rats find electric shocks to their feet very unpleasant, and will go to great lengths to avoid them. In one experiment, rats were given some control over their plight: if they pushed a lever, they would be shocked less frequently than before. A second group of rats received a shock whenever the first ones did, but could do nothing to control the situation. Rats in this powerless position produced more corticosterone (equivalent to cortisol in humans) and were more likely to develop ulcers than the lever-pushing ones, even though they experienced the same number of stressful shocks. Giving control and then taking it away can have even greater consequences. Rats were trained to press a lever to avoid a shock, then prevented from doing so when a shock was expected. These rats showed a stress response even if they did not receive a shock.

The dimension of control turns out to be more important than anything else in modulating hormonal responses to stress. Stress researchers – notably Seymour Levine at Stanford University in California – define control as the individual's capacity to do something to change the environment during the presence of something harmful or unpleasant.[19] This sense of control can account for the observation that experienced air-traffic controllers and drivers of heavy goods vehicles – people engaged in ostensibly stressful tasks – do not apparently show elevated levels of stress hormones on the job.

Predictability also lessens stress, while uncertainty increases it. Rats given a warning before a shock produced far less corticosterone than rats given a shock with no warning – presumably because the rats given warnings could relax their vigilance in between times. Animals subjected to prolonged exposure to unpredictable and uncontrollable stressful experiences develop what researchers have called 'learned helplessness' – they more or less give up on life.

Thus physiologists themselves argue that to reduce the stressfulness of an event for a particular individual, it must be made predictable and controllable. Yet people under stress in their daily lives are routinely offered Valium or training in 'stress management'. They are advised to seek inner solutions for what is essentially a problem about the way the world is currently constituted.

'Managing' Stress at Work

A conference in 1985 organised by the Coronary Prevention Group in London and devoted to the question 'Does stress cause heart attacks?' highlighted the current contradictions.[20] Addressing the issue of occupational stress, a lone trade unionist, David Gee, put the case for an alternative approach. Evidence is strong, he argued, that such stress is caused by little or no control of the job. The solution lies in 'an extension of democracy at work', and legislation along Swedish lines to ensure that 'the employee himself can influence his work situation'.

Yet Colin Mackay of the Health and Safety Executive – addressing 'the prevention of stress at work' – talked of counselling, psychotherapy, relaxation therapy, 'alteration of cognitive appraisal', 'cognitive restructuring', and 'personality difficulties or inappropriateness of training or personal skills'. Discounting the popular myth that only senior executives suffer stress at work, Mackay pointed to increasing evidence that even 'simple, repetitive shop-floor jobs' can be stressful. Assuming that this is a symptom of the failure of 'man–job fit', he suggested that it might be necessary to instigate selection procedures even for unskilled jobs. By showing signs of stress, the workers have proved themselves to be misfits; they have 'failed to match the demands' of their work. The fault lies in the worker, not the workplace.

Meanwhile, the managers too are suffering in silence. At the conference, Aubrey Jones, of Hoover plc, said that managers keep quiet because they 'equate being stressed with failing to cope'. He was not optimistic that things would improve. 'Where then are the answers? There are no answers. The game will not change,' he concluded. Stress is apparently impossible to escape; it is something you must simply 'come to terms with' in silence, alone.

Yet some people deliberately stress themselves: the devotees of rock-climbing, hang-gliding and bungee-jumping, for instance, take delight in experiencing stress combined with control – they feel most alive as they take action to save themselves from perilous situations.[21] This demonstrates that it is not stressful situations that people find so aversive, but being powerless to effect any change.

The Gendering of Stress

In the political climate of the 1990s, with the decline in the trade unions' power to effect changes in the workplace, many citizens may feel less and less able to alter the way things are, and more and more stressed in sometimes inchoate ways. But the burdens fall particularly heavily on women, not least because the concept of stress is itself gendered. The growing individualisation of experience, and the incessant focus on taking responsibility for managing your own body, have particularly negative consequences for women. Women are regarded as being responsible for managing the stress experienced by other people – their partners, children, work colleagues, even friends and acquaintances – yet these tasks are rarely seen as an extra source of stress for the woman herself. Stress at work is typically perceived as something that men suffer from; their wives or partners are charged with managing their private lives to ensure that they have plenty of opportunity to relax and unwind, engage in healthy sporting activities and the like, while women's 'leisure' time may be severely restricted. Stress has even been used to explain men's violence towards women, according to Jalna Hanmer and Jeff Hearn at Bradford University. 'In this view, women are stressed but cause stress.'[22]

It is acknowledged that women experience stress too, but this is rarely regarded as being the important, life-threatening sort from which men in high-status employment are said to suffer. If women are enjoined to manage their stress, it is primarily for the benefit of others, and in order to remain attractive and youthful. A recent issue of *BBC Good Health* magazine told women: 'Beat Stress to Boost Beauty'.[23] Even a short time of excessive stress, the magazine warned, 'can play havoc with our looks'. Insomnia takes the greatest toll on the skin: deprived of the rejuvenating hormones most active during sleep, 'the skin soon takes on a sallow and devitalised look'. Readers are enjoined to follow a 'seven-day anti-stress beauty plan', with daily sessions of meditation and 'body brushing', which is guaranteed to 'help to restore natural good looks'.

Popular health books, as well as scientific works, emphasise that the influence of hormones on bodily functions is intimately tied up with what an individual thinks, feels and experiences. Hormone levels rise and fall in response to what we eat, what exercise we take, whether we are calm or distraught. Self-help books in particular aim to give their readers an enhanced sense of control over the inner workings of their bodies, but paradoxically may have the opposite effect. Now we need to manage not only our bodies but our very thoughts and emotions, for fear of disrupting our hormonal balance and succumbing to the dire effects of stress.

Regarding hormones as exquisitely sensitive to social influences is not necessarily empowering, as Sally Shuttleworth and others have pointed out.[24] Victorian doctors, too, stressed the impact of the social on the physical. They put enormous stress on the lability of the menstrual flow, and advised their patients to sacrifice all intellectual endeavour and emotional excitement on the altar of healthy menses. Pregnant women were also urged to stay calm for nine months and do nothing that might excite their passions, to safeguard the fetus from their raging inner chemistry – an idea echoed in much contemporary advice for pregnant women, Shuttleworth argues.[25]

The sexual politics underlying ideas about stress become

obvious only when the links with social inequalities and the organisation of work are acknowledged. Arlie Hochschild's widely cited study of women flight attendants in the United States, described in her book *The Managed Heart*, reveals further twists in the gender and stress story.[26] Air 'hostesses' are required by their employers to manage their emotions in order to produce the smiling facial expressions and bodily postures that convey feminine reassurance, ready availability and dutiful servility. The stress they suffered from the demanding physical work was greatly exacerbated by the requirement to behave in this particular way, which Hochschild dubbed 'emotion work'. To cope with the demands made upon them without losing their self-respect, most women opted for what Hochschild calls 'deep acting' – suppressing any feelings of anger or irritation at rude, aggressive or demanding passengers, for instance, by thinking up reasons to feel sympathy and understanding for those particular passengers. This enabled the flight attendants to avoid feeling insincere, but only at the cost of feeling alienated from their own bodily expressions and emotions – the result of always having to block their normal emotional responses and work at developing alternatives. The stress even shows on their bodies: the constant smiling eventually creates permanent lines on the women's faces.

Is Aggression in Men's Hormones?

One night in September 1986, a young man in his twenties, out joy-riding with his friends, picked up a hitchhiker in West Palm Beach, Florida. The night ended with the brutal murder of the hitchhiker. The young man, Horace Williams, was described by friends and family as a nice kid – kind, considerate, and a regular churchgoer. A year or so before the crime, however, he had taken up bodybuilding, and developed an obsessive interest in it. He was also taking anabolic steroids – artificial hormones related to testosterone. At the trial, his lawyer argued that the hormones had rendered him legally insane and incapable of appreciating the consequences or wrongfulness of his acts. The jury, unswayed by the lawyer's plea, found Williams guilty.[27]

Nevertheless, many scientists and non-scientists alike believe that hormones, especially that quintessentially 'male' one, testosterone, can explain why men are more likely than women to cause physical damage to other human beings. At the extreme, eight or nine murderers out of ten are male. Does testosterone really make men more aggressive than women? Can hormones turn people into violent killers?

Adolf Hitler seems to have thought so. He is credited with being one of the first users of testosterone – first synthesised in 1935 – and reputedly prescribed it for his troops.[28] But research into the link between testosterone and human aggression has failed to come up with a consistent picture. One recent study, for instance, claimed that anabolic steroids make men more angry and aggressive. But the researchers had asked the bodybuilders themselves to describe the effects – an approach that is notoriously open to bias from what individuals believe the drugs will do to them. In other studies, in which steroid-taking athletes also said the drugs made them more aggressive, a range of psychological tests failed to reveal any sign of this. Men who decide to use steroids may also be more aggressive than most in the first place. As a result, no firm conclusions can be drawn from a recent study of steroid abusers attending a needle exchange clinic in Wales which reported 'heightened aggressiveness' among the steroid injectors. Yet the study was reported with headlines such as 'Steroids Can Turn Athletes Into Killers'.[29]

Aggression is enduringly seen as a drive or instinct that can burst out at any time, in any context. But it is a gendered drive – it is accepted, albeit deplored, in men, as part of masculinity. The stiffest punishments are typically meted out to women who are aggressive in what are regarded as inappropriate circumstances.

Yet the theory that aggression is an instinct fuelled by inner chemicals that build up and eventually burst through the floodgates is difficult to substantiate in studies of humans and other animals alike. Even when animals are motivated to fight, attack is not a simple reflex response to a stimulus, argues Felicity Huntingford of the University of Glasgow:[30] 'Whether or not two potential opponents come to blows depends on a complex assessment of their probability of winning or of being injured and of the value of the disputed resource.' Such judgements are made during long displays – spiders raise and vibrate their walking legs, fish raise their gill covers, red deer stags roar and strut about – which may, only gradually, escalate into physical contact. In the wild, fights are usually resolved by one animal withdrawing before either participant has suffered any damage.

Scientists such as Huntingford argue that hormones are merely a part of the bodily mechanism which enables humans and other animals to be aggressive, just as limbs enable them to walk. It is a mistake to think of hormones as somehow controlling the display of aggression. In humans, just as in monkeys and mice, most attempts to link testosterone levels to aggressive behaviour have failed. In every species that has been studied, including humans, scientists conclude, the concentrations of testosterone in the blood 'do not correlate with the extent of their aggressiveness nor predict their success in aggressive encounters'.[31]

Why the Testosterone Myth?

A plausible biochemical explanation of the persistent myth that testosterone is to blame for male violence is the fact that long-term heavy drinking seems to raise testosterone levels, at least in young men. A recent study showed that when alcohol abuse was controlled, there was no significant relationship between testosterone, or eight other hormones, and aggressive tendencies. This suggests that it is the alcohol, not the hormones, which increases the likelihood of violence.[32] But even this finding must be placed in a wider context. Mark Rosenberg, an epidemiologist at the Centers for Disease Control in Atlanta, has carried out a statistical analysis of violence in America. It shows that violence almost always happens between people who knew each other, are drinking, and have fallen into an argument. If there is a gun about, chances are that someone will be killed.[33]

Brain research may also have encouraged popular belief in the inevitability of male aggression. As the testosterone theory waned, researchers moved on to the brain, hoping to unravel the 'neural systems' involved in aggression. Such work hit the headlines in the late 1960s when Jose Delgado demonstrated his angry cats.[34] He implanted radio receivers in the brains of cats and monkeys, and showed that he could cause them to attack another animal by stimulating the hypothalamus. Delgado's work has inspired many horrific science-fiction stories depicting people with electrodes planted in their brains controlled by the possessor of the radiotransmitter.

In the 1950s and 1960s neurosurgeons operated on what they thought were the 'aggression centres' in the brains of scores of disturbed patients. These operations damaged parts of the brain, sometimes destroying an individual's ability to form new memories, but did not have much effect on aggressive behaviour. 'There does not appear to be any simple aggression centre in the [human] brain,' Ronald Langevin at the Clarke Institute of Psychiatry at the University of Toronto concluded recently.[35]

Scientists now expect to find brain chemicals linked to aggression. Research pharmacologists claim that a new class of anti-aggressive drugs, described as 'serenics', are on the horizon; they will act by increasing the level of one of the brain's neurotransmitters, serotonin.[36] Neuroscientists are on the trail of protein fragments known as peptides, which apparently induce aggression when they are released in the right part of the brain.[37] But will the discovery of a new sort of tranquilliser or an 'aggressivity' peptide explain human aggression? As Jeffrey Goldstein, a psychologist at Temple University in Philadelphia, argues, we would still need to determine how social and psychological events trigger the chemical cascade in the brain. In the natural, electrode- and drug-free brain, 'it is cognitive and environmental factors that are themselves responsible for the stimulation in the first instance'. The odd thing about people, Goldstein claims, is that we can so readily behave aggressively because of the beliefs we hold.[38]

None of this is to deny the reality of brain chemicals or hormones, or the fact that they are brought into play when someone behaves aggressively. The point is that it makes no sense to seek a biological explanation for acts of aggression, in isolation from the social and cultural embeddedness of individuals throughout their lifetime.

An example comes from Hochschild's book *The Managed Heart*.[39] Hochschild also studied debt collectors, the epitome of a gendered profession, whose job it is to instil anxiety and fear in clients. The emotion work these men do – having to behave in an aggressive way – can spill over into the rest of their lives, Hochschild found. Hostility and anger became emotions frequently felt and displayed towards their partners and children.

Culture also plays a powerful part in shaping aggressive behaviour. Anthropologists have produced examples of societies where men and women are regarded as equally agreeable and peaceable, and others where males seem extraordinarily violent, even by Western standards. Always, cultural expectations of who will be violent, and why, seem to influence what people do. One example makes the point. The phrase 'running amok' comes from a pattern of homicidal violence once relatively common in Malaysia, Indonesia and New Guinea.[40] In a typical outburst, a man would first go through a period of brooding after an insult or blow to his self-esteem, then strike out indiscriminately against kin and strangers, killing several, until finally he lapsed into exhaustion and amnesia. Lances were kept in public places in the event of an 'amok runner'. This behaviour was regarded as deviant, yet it is patterned on behaviours esteemed in the culture. The term *amok* comes from the war cry of the medieval Malaysian warrior, still a heroic figure in popular culture. Running amok, though it is rare today, still enjoys a certain tacit social approbation in these cultures, much like Jesse James and other cowboy killers in the contemporary United States.

The evidence in favour of the importance of social and cultural factors in male aggressiveness is now so strong that what is in need of explanation is why so much research effort is still devoted to finding a biological cause. A recent book by Deborah Denno, *Biology and Violence: From Birth to Adulthood*, is an example of the new 'biologism'.[41] Following a thousand black people living in inner-city Philadelphia from birth to the age of twenty-two, the author attempts to relate variation in police contact to a hundred variables including handedness, physical growth, lead intoxication, birth trauma and minor physical anomalies, such as small head circumference, and the shape and position of the eyes.

Appealing 'Imperatives'

There is much at stake in maintaining the notion that men are inevitably more aggressive than women. Sometimes this is used as a justification for male hostility to the prospect of equality between the sexes. Just how this argument works is beautifully displayed in *The Fragile Male* by Ben Greenstein.[42] A South African pharmacist who retrained as a biologist in Britain, and now studies the hormonal basis of rheumatoid arthritis in a London hospital, Greenstein is convinced that men are condemned to aggression and sexual violence because of their hormones. Greenstein argues: 'The plight of women can be ascribed to a single chemical, the male sex hormone, testosterone. This one hormone . . . sealed her fate for millions of years . . .' Now, we have civilisation, moral codes, the ability to 'work towards ironing out differences which in the past have stimulated discord, conflict, exploitation and open warfare', he acknowledges. But Greenstein's mission is to argue that good will never triumph, because 'the biological imperative is inflexible'. Greenstein claims that the human male is 'driven by forces that will not be denied', forces that make his 'thoughts, wills and actions' outside his control. Feminists are thus on dangerous ground and can expect a violent reaction: thanks to civilisation, 'men can no longer function as untrammelled males, and women seem to them to be taking away what little they have left'. Reviewing *The Fragile Male* in *The Sunday Telegraph*, David Sexton spells out Greenstein's argument: 'Since it is simply a mistake to think that there can ever be a "New Man", all the stresses of the sex war, including the rise in rape, are therefore the fault of women.' He quotes Greenstein's final ultimatum: 'Man is a fact of life, there is no changing him either through books or laws, and women can either come to terms with this or intensify the sex war.'[43]

Even women can find solace in the idea that men are intrinsically more aggressive than women. Writing in *The Sunday Telegraph* about 'women's long fight for equality', Minette Marrin argues:

> There is growing scientific evidence about the functioning of the brain which suggests women tend to be less assertive and aggressive than men. What most of us suffer from is not so much the barrier of a 'glass ceiling' but a hormonal handicap which makes it difficult for us to smash it. Many able women do not even want to try and are short of the killer instinct which everyone needs to get to the top.[44]

A way out of this impasse – with some commentators stressing social and cultural components, while others continue to search for biological causes – is to work towards the development of a more complex model of the ways in which human bodies, experiences and emotions are interconnected. In recent years sociologists have begun to devise theoretical frameworks that can begin to make sense of our experience – developments recently reviewed by Chris Shilling in his book *The Body and Social Theory*.[45] The work of Peter Freund – to give just one example – shows that it is not impossible to begin to think along these lines.[46] He argues that emotions arise out of interactions with others, with unpleasant emotions centring around situations in which individuals are disempowered. This experience in turn has implications for bodily functions and our ability to achieve a sense of bodily well-being. Damaging social conditions could conceivably result in a long-term alteration in an individual's brain chemistry, as some have claimed, making them more prone to certain kinds of emotional responses in the future.

Emotional ways of being are differentiated along social lines, Freund points out, with implications for our ability to achieve bodily well-being. An individual's social and economic position influences, in complex ways, the way a person's body functions at many levels (just as malnutrition occasioned by poverty leads to stunted physical growth). In this view, bodily responses such as aggression are learnt just as much as language is; both processes rely on bodies that are primed in particular ways, but neither is a matter solely of either nature or nurture. The processes that shape the body and its capabilities are social; such processes, in turn, are continually transformed by the deployment of these capabilities in the social arena. Hormones, or even brain chemicals, cannot carry the conceptual weight required to describe and explain what it means to be an embodied self enmeshed in a social web.

Patsy Rodenburg, head of the voice department at the Royal National Theatre and the Guildhall School of Music and Drama, argues that violence would decline if more people could 'speak up' for themselves: 'Some of the students I've had, who've come from very violent backgrounds, now tell me they feel they can talk about something rather than physically exploding. If you don't have words, what are you to do?'[47] As biologists Felicity Huntingford and Angela Turner conclude: 'The means of preventing and controlling human aggression are available to us, but they are sociological and political, rather than biological in nature.'[48]

Yet even those who believe that testosterone is the root of rape and war do not argue for chemical remedies. No one seriously suggests that men should take antiandrogens to make them more placid. Dosing a woman with hormones – even 'male' ones – is far easier for most doctors to countenance than any tinkering with a man's hormonal status; even a British sex offender who recently pleaded for castration was denied the operation by his doctors, and their decision was upheld in court.

'Appropriate' behavior differs for men and women. Men can legitimately behave in threatening ways, and hormonal accounts of male behaviour often reflect this sense of brooding menace. But it is typically women who are expected to manage the supposed behavioural consequences of male hormones. When something 'goes wrong' for a man, the 'failure of control' is rarely seen as exclusively his own.

4

HORMONES ON THE BRAIN

THE SECRET OF SEXUAL DIFFERENCE?

'W hen you first meet a human being, the first distinction you make is "male or female?" and you are accustomed to make the distinction with unhesitating certainty,' wrote Sigmund Freud in 1933.[1] Anything that threatens that certainty makes most people nervous. Today, even disposable nappies come colour-coded, blue for boys and pink for girls, with anatomically correct areas of maximum padding. When, a few years ago, a *New York Times* journalist reported that before the First World War boy babies were dressed in pink, described as 'a stronger, more decided colour', and girls in 'delicate' and 'dainty' blue, many readers were 'casually astonished', writes Marjorie Garber in her book on transvestites and transsexuals, *Vested Interests: Cross-Dressing and Cultural Anxiety*.[2] To the consternation of many, a cultural practice usually taken for granted was suddenly revealed to be arbitrary.

As part of modern culture, science too is eager to translate difference into inevitability by constructing theories that offer to explain how such difference arose. The marriage of endocrinology and brain science has produced a now vibrant young offspring: the theory that most – if not all – the differences we note in the way women and men are have their origins in the hormonal environments individuals experienced while they were still fetuses in their mothers' wombs. This theory claims to account for the observation that few women are mathematicians or physicists, and few men are nurses or childminders, or the fact that boys play football while girls play with dolls. It purports to explain why some people have lovers of the same sex, while others pair up with members of the opposite sex. It claims to reveal what makes us masculine or feminine, and what makes us fall in love with another human being. Its critics claim that it stigmatises feminists and homosexuals as hormonal deviants, so undercutting their claims to equal rights, and threatens to give us all an impoverished sense of what sexuality is all about.

Rats, Guinea Pigs, Genitalia and Gender

This remarkable theory of what amounts to 'womb programming' grew from the discovery, in the 1940s, that, among mammals, a genetically male fetus needs a supply of androgen hormone in the womb if it is to develop male genitals. Without that, individuals of either genetic sex develop a female reproductive system. Everything works smoothly most of the time, because a fetus that is genetically male develops testicles, which in turn secrete the testosterone hormone needed to develop a male's reproductive equipment.

Some scientists went on to speculate that a fetus's brain, not just its body, might acquire a 'sex' in the womb. They argued that the developing brain might be prenatally imprinted – by a particular cocktail of hormones – along masculine or feminine lines. Depending on what happened before birth, an individual would later think or act in either masculine or feminine ways. This hormonal imprinting, they reasoned, could also determine whether an individual will be sexually attracted to members of the same or the opposite sex.

A classic animal experiment forged the foundations of these ideas. In 1959 Charles Phoenix and his colleagues at the

University of Kansas injected testosterone into pregnant guinea pigs.[3] They created baby guinea pigs which were genetically female but nonetheless had penises. And these anomalous infants not only looked like males, they behaved sexually rather like them too. They mounted other guinea pigs more frequently than untreated females did, and were less likely to adopt the typical female mating posture, an arching of the back known as lordosis. Phoenix and his colleagues concluded that the infant females' brains, not just their bodies, had been irreversibly masculinised by the hormonal manipulations. Exposure to androgens in the womb has an 'organising action' on the brain, he and his co-workers claimed, permanently altering adult sexual behaviour.

At the time, most scientists readily accepted the 'organisational theory'. The hormonal programming of the brain was deemed irreversible, just as the genital anatomy had proved to be. Later in life, everyone agreed, hormonal changes could only activate the prenatally imprinted programme: neither social expectations nor experiences in childhood or adulthood could alter this inner 'brain sex'.

Today, this picture is considerably more blurred. Even a rat's brain and behaviour appear to be more flexible, and more influenced by their environment, than researchers had supposed.[4] Nerve cells can increase in number and size, grow new projections, and remodel their connections with other neurons in response to a range of hormones throughout life. A rat's social and physical context can also profoundly alter regions of the brain purported to differ inexorably between the sexes. Simply housing rats in groups with interesting objects to play with, rather than keeping them isolated in standard uniform cages, can influence both the degree and even the direction of sex differences in many 'cognitive' areas of the brain such as the hippocampus and the cerebral cortex. And even in rodents, sexual behaviour shifts dramatically, depending on the context. Female hamsters kept in cages on their own apparently do not engage in male-style mounting of other hamsters, even given the opportunity, but female hamsters which live in social groups with other females do frequently mount one another. Thus researchers are beginning to acknowledge that an animal's social setting has a profound effect upon its behaviour.[5]

Moreover, even 'normal' male and female rodents happily indulge in the thrusting activities mistakenly deemed the preserve of the male. One of the most painstaking studies of rat sexuality in recent years was conducted by two Mexican researchers, Gabriela Morali and Carlos Beyer.[6] To study the fine detail of penile–vaginal interactions, they placed an acceleration transducer on the male's back, wired up to an oscilloscope. This device picks up the male's thrusting, recording it as peaks and troughs on an electronic trace, as the transducer is alternately moved forwards and backwards.

This ingenious technology demonstrates that females are perfectly capable of behaving like males. They happily mount other rats and go through all the motions, just as if they were males. Researchers in the 1950s suggested that this should be called 'pseudo-male' behaviour, implying that the behaviour is somehow not the same as the male's. Yet research over several decades on rats, dogs, sheep, rabbits and guinea pigs has consistently shown that male and pseudo-male behaviour are identical. The Mexicans' machinery confirmed that female and male rats are indistinguishable in both the vigour and the frequency of their thrusting. 'A longer duration of mounts in females was the only significant difference between the sexes,' they report.

The researchers then tried to see what happened when they altered the hormonal status of the animals by first removing their testicles or ovaries, then treating them with oestrogen or testosterone. They manipulated both newborn and adult rats in this way. But altering the rats' hormones had virtually no effect on their copulatory movements. The researchers conclude that the 'neural substrate for thrusting develops independently of hormones'.

Most telling of all, perhaps, is the suggestion that even in rats, social experience influences sexual behaviour as adults. For some years, Celia Moore and her colleagues have garnered evidence that it is the mother rat's response to her pups that is crucial. Moore and her colleagues have shown that mother rats lick the genital region of male pups more than that of females, and that the amount of licking a pup receives influences its sexual behaviour as an adult.[7] It turns out that testosterone excreted in the urine stimulates the mother's attention. Female pups treated with testosterone get more attention, while castrated males are ignored. Pups that receive more anogenital licking are later more likely to mount other rats, regardless of their genetic sex. Moore discovered that she could mimic the maternal effect simply by stroking female pups with a paintbrush each day. Females stimulated in this way developed masculine behaviour, and their pituitary gland, at the base of the brain, functioned in a male style too.

Moore's work is rarely cited, however, by supporters of 'brain sex'. But when it is – as in *The Sexual Brain* by Simon LeVay, a neuroanatomist at the Salk Institute, San Diego – her findings are seen as a 'bizarre chain of events'.[8] Further research is needed, LeVay says, to explain why male infant rats should require this 'validation' of their maleness from their mothers to achieve normal male rat sexuality, when, he claims, nature could so easily have arranged for a fixed internal programme to do the trick. Moore's findings do not convey to him the message feminist biologists have received: that even in rats, sexuality is not determined in the womb.

Many decades ago, the pioneering American behavioural endocrinologist Frank Beach gently informed his colleagues that humans, unlike rats, do not show highly specific masculine and feminine motor patterns of copulation. In 1950, in a classic paper entitled 'The Snark was a Boojum', he warned of the dangers of overenthusiastic extrapolation from rat mating to human sexuality. With rats as surrogate humans, Beach cautioned, an understanding of human sexuality and gender would prove elusive.[9]

Yet in the closing years of the twentieth century, there are still many who do not heed his advice. From neuroanatomists such as LeVay, right through to psychologists who work at levels far removed from the details of brain development or molecular function, scientists continue to base their research on simplistic animal models which do not even adequately reflect the way animals function. The traditional animal data – the classic experiments – are ceremoniously paraded in paper after paper as the apparent justification for an idea they seem reluctant to relinquish, no matter how threadbare: the presumption that hormones in the womb can unproblematically define a person's 'brain sex'.

Hormones for Map-reading

The idea of 'brain sex', the notion that all the traits we typically associate with a particular gender – from genitalia to an interest in train-spotting or sewing – could all be tied neatly together in what one researcher called a 'coherent set' by sex hormones in the womb seems to be irresistibly attractive to many scientists in the field. A good example of this kind of thinking comes from the research on sex differences in human spatial ability.

The results of this research have already percolated into everyday life. The findings are often cited to explain why post-adolescent girls and women tend to steer clear of mathematics, or why women supposedly make bad drivers. 'Women are probably safer drivers than men because they are less aggressive, but my personal experience is that women drivers are more likely to make errors in judgement,' an Australian science journalist, Graeme O'Neill, confidently expounded in the *Melbourne Age* recently. In support, he quoted contemporary psychological research: 'Men's greater spatial awareness and ability to perceive and compensate for relative motion and speed might account for this.'[10]

Doreen Kimura is at the forefront of such research today. *Scientific American* recently described her as 'a petite woman in her fifties whose stature belies her toughness'.[11] Kimura grew up in a small town in Saskatchewan, and worked before entering McGill University as a mature student. There she acquired her lifelong interest in the brain from Donald O. Hebb, one of the first to attempt to trace the neural basis of learning. Kimura is impervious to feminist critiques which argue that research on hormones and sex differences feeds prejudice against women. She told her interviewer: 'You have to think you are right when everyone tells you you're wrong. You can't be acquiescent and do science.' She added: 'My interest is in finding out how the brain really works. I don't have any ax to grind, political or otherwise.'

In her pencil-and-paper tests, girls and women on average score higher on verbal tasks, while boys and men tend to do better on spatial tasks (which often require you to rotate or fold up objects in your imagination). Kimura denies that experiences in childhood could account for these apparently different mental abilities. She believes that such cognitive differences in the way individuals think, reason and remember are caused by sex hormones in the womb, which somehow – and irrevocably – programme the way a person's brain works in adulthood.

In a typical test, conducted in Kimura's laboratory, a group of North American university undergraduates were asked to study a table-top map and learn a particular route. Men reportedly learnt the route in fewer trials and made fewer errors than did women. But once learning was complete, women apparently remembered more of the landmarks than men did. From findings like this, Kimura and others have speculated that men do 'better' because their brains evolved to navigate on long-distance trips as they searched for game or mates. Women did not evolve such skills, because they stayed at home minding the baby. They had only to find their way around the cave and its immediate environment with the help of local landmarks.[12]

Kimura and like-minded colleagues have gone on to predict that this evolutionary grand plan is played out through hormonal differences between the sexes. In this view, the more testosterone you've got, the higher you should score on a spatial ability test.

But in 1983 Valerie Shute of the University of California at Santa Barbara and her colleagues got some peculiar results from their college student volunteers.[13] Among women, the high-androgen subjects were better at the spatial tests; in men, the reverse was true: low-androgen men outperformed the high-androgen ones. Kimura and her colleague Catherine Gouchie have carried out similar tests of spatial ability and mathematical reasoning, with similar results.[14] Such findings suggest, Kimura concludes, that there is some 'optimum level' of testosterone for 'maximal spatial ability'. But this level seems to fall in the 'low male range' – typical, for instance, of men with small testicles due to a rare genetic disorder known as Klinefelter's syndrome. These findings look like a serious blow to the hormonal explanation of men's relative success on spatial ability, but Kimura refuses to relinquish her hypothesis. More research is needed, she urges, to reveal 'the precise mechanisms' at play.

Women are reputed to be more manually dextrous, surpassing men when asked to place pegs quickly into holes or assemble bits of metal in a certain order. According to anthropologist Helen Fisher, ancestral women evolved this skill because they needed to pick berries out of the dense vegetation. Kimura admits that 'the female advantage in such tasks may be at least partly related to their smaller finger size', in the wake of a study which showed that 'marked sex differences on a fine motor skill task' disappeared when the researchers controlled for the size of people's fingers.[15] Yet she concludes that the central nervous system, prenatally primed by hormones, 'contributes' to the scores.

Some researchers have contested the very claim that there are sex differences in spatial skills. When Paula Caplan at the University of Toronto reviewed the literature in this field, she uncovered such a morass of conflicting methodologies and findings that she doubts whether there is something that can legitimately be called spatial ability, definable outside the examination room; certainly there are no grounds for concluding that men have superior spatial skills.[16]

But even if the results of spatial ability tests are taken at face value, their significance remains in doubt. First, the overlap between the sexes is large, so most men and women perform equally well on these tests. Secondly, the differences are small, and they apply only to populations, not to individuals. The chances are that any given man or woman would score similarly on these tests. Moreover, researchers normally sample a very limited range of humanity – typically, white American college students – yet the data are often projected beyond this.

What is more, performance seems to change over time. Some reported sex differences in test scores – among North American secondary school students, at least – have disappeared; others are less pronounced.[17] This makes it probable that these tests reflect acquired knowledge and skill rather than innate ability. (A cautionary tale comes from the Harvard biologist Stephen Jay Gould, who has shown how Alfred Binet's original IQ tests, which were specifically intended to measure performance, not innate ability, were transformed by an influential school of American psychologists into tools for measuring inherited mental ability.[18])

The most important point remains: we do not have to look far for alternative explanations of difference that are far more plausible than hormonal programming *in utero*. In most cultures, boys and girls are treated in very different ways, and encouraged to behave in very different ways; from their first months of life, girls and boys have very different experiences of the world. Barbara Lloyd, professor of social psychology at the University of Sussex, has shown that adults even handle newborn infants in distinctly different ways, depending on whether they think they are boys or girls. (She dressed babies in blue or pink and watched what happened.[19]) As Ruth Hubbard of Harvard University and others have argued, there is a kind of dialectical interaction – what Hubbard calls a transformation – in the interplay between biological and cultural factors, which makes it impossible to separate the two:

If a society puts half its children in dresses and skirts but warns them not to move in ways that reveal their underpants, while putting the other half in jeans and overalls and encouraging them to climb trees and play ball and other active outdoor games; if later, during adolescence, the half that has worn trousers is exhorted to 'eat like a growing boy,' while the half in skirts is warned to watch its weight and not get fat; if the half in jeans trots around in sneakers or boots, while the half in skirts totters about on spike heels, then these two groups of people will be biologically as well as socially different. Their muscles will be different, as will their reflexes, posture, arms, legs and feet, hand–eye coordination, spatial perception, and so on. They will also be biologically different if, as adults, they spend eight hours a day sitting in front of a visual display terminal or work on a construction job or in a mine.[20]

The Anatomy of Brain Sex

Undaunted, the supporters of hormonal programming in the womb as the origin of differences between the sexes claim that the structure of the brain supports their view. They say that differential exposure to hormones before birth has led to sex differences in the way tasks are apportioned to different bits of the brain.

In most people, the left side of the brain's cerebral cortex is largely responsible for speech: this is an example of what is called cerebral specialisation or lateralisation of function. But not everyone conforms to this picture. In many left-handed people, for instance, the right side of the brain also apparently has something to do with the ability to speak. A popular idea at the moment is that men are more lateralised than women; women are meant to show less specialisation. In women, both sides of the brain might contribute to the control of speech, for instance.

But a confusing array of observations, mostly of people with various sorts of brain damage, rather spoils this picture. Few researchers now claim that everything is less lateralised in the female brain. Some functions are said to be more diffusely organised in women; others more diffusely organised in men. Researchers have also found sex differences between the front and back of the brain. Yet no one can suggest how any of these supposed differences in brain organisation might translate into behaviour.[21]

Several neuroscientists have also reported sex differences in the physical structure of the brain. Dick Swaab and his colleagues were the first to discover, in 1985, a cluster of brain cells – the so-called sexually dimorphic nucleus – which is apparently bigger in males than in females.[22] But later, in 1988, the researchers established that the differences arise not in fetal life but in childhood. Only after the age of two or three did a difference between males and females appear. This difference in the size of the brain cell cluster was the result of a decrease in cell number in the female's nucleus, but not in the male's. In men, the number of cells in the nucleus declines sharply after the age of forty-five. So sexual differentiation of the human brain must continue after birth – where, Swaab concludes, it could be influenced not just by 'chemical and hormonal factors' but also by 'social factors'.

In other words, even if this sexually dimorphic nucleus in the brain has something to do with the differences in the way men and women typically behave (for which there is no evidence), the divergent brain anatomy Swaab reports could be the result of social experience in early childhood; it is certainly not determined in the womb.

What significance any of this has for differences in human behaviour is far from clear. In rat and human alike, the function of the sexually dimorphic nucleus is not known. Equally mysterious are the anatomical sex differences reported in other regions of the brain – the corpus callosum, the superior cervical ganglion, the amygdala, the dorsal hippocampus and the orbital frontal cortex. Moreover, in discussions of these anatomical details, one crucial lacuna in the evidence is often overlooked: no one has linked any human anatomical brain difference to any hormonal event in the womb.[23] Nor has molecular dissection of the brain so far revealed significant differences between the sexes. Both sexes have the brain enzymes needed to convert androgens into oestrogens. The receptors, or cellular docking sites, for these two hormones are also distributed throughout the brain in identical patterns. The same is true for the receptors sensitive to the hormone progesterone, the so-called hormone of pregnancy. As the endocrinologist Etienne Baulieu puts it, 'several important pieces of machinery transmitting sexual information are similar or identical in the two sexes and so probably do not explain sex differences in behaviour'.[24]

Girls 'Masculinised' in the Womb?

When scientists lament the lack of rigorous data on the human condition, they blame ethical constraints. But even if they could easily measure hormone levels in the womb, they would have to keep track of the offspring for the rest of their lives to find out what their sex life was like, or whether they became a defence industry engineer, say, rather than a nurse. So researchers in search of evidence for a link between prenatal hormones and adult lifestyle have leapt upon 'experiments of nature' – people who were exposed to an altered hormonal environment in the womb as a result of some spontaneous endocrine disorders. The two most common conditions are known as androgen insensitivity syndrome (androgen is the general term for testosterone and other male hormones) and congenital adrenal hyperplasia – a genetic mishap affecting the hormones from the adrenal glands. People born with these disorders have had every nook and cranny of their psyche thoroughly inspected. Scores of researchers have investigated not just their IQ, but also their jobs, their hobbies, their attitudes to marriage and motherhood, and their sex lives.

Children with androgen insensitivity syndrome are born with female or ambiguous external genitalia, although they are genetically male. Often reared as girls, they are usually discovered by the medical profession only when they do not begin to menstruate. They have abdominal testes that produce testosterone, but their tissues are completely insensitive to it. They look female, and develop breasts at puberty, because they retain the normal biochemical pathway that enables cells to convert testosterone to oestradiol.

Two American researchers, John Money at Johns Hopkins Hospital in Baltimore and Anke Ehrhardt of the State University of New York at Buffalo, along with many colleagues, have studied these children since the 1950s.[25] They have discovered that affected individuals develop a female gender identity and a sexual orientation towards men. No one could fault their 'femininity'. Some researchers would like to conclude from this that an 'androgen-deficient prenatal environment' determined their sexual interest in men as adults, but concede that here 'the effects of rearing and hormones are confounded'. So no conclusions can be drawn on the relative importance of prenatal hormones or upbringing on gender identity or sexual orientation.

Congenital adrenal hyperplasia, or CAH, is an enzyme defect which results in most of the steroid hormone produced by the adrenal cortex being transformed from corticosteroid into androgen. Either genetic sex can have this syndrome. Infant girls with CAH are sometimes born with masculinised genitalia, usually resembling a penis and scrotum so closely that some are considered for a time to be boys. Most have surgery in later life to reconstruct the clitoris, labia and vagina. All individuals with CAH require lifelong treatment with cortisone to compensate for their non-functioning adrenal glands.

Ehrhardt and her colleagues found that if they were reared as girls, CAH individuals developed female gender identity. But most of them exhibited 'tomboyism' – defined as a preference for outdoor active play over indoor, less active play. These girls also showed more interest in a public career than in being a housewife, and less interest in tending small infants and playing with dolls, than 'normal' young females. In a later study, Money and Ehrhardt reported that 37 per cent of the CAH girls rated themselves homosexual or bisexual. Those raised as boys had a male gender identity and apparently conventional sexual orientations.[26]

Girls Will Be Girls: The Shifting Sands of Gender

Critiques of this research have highlighted various shortcomings. Other researchers have failed to replicate one of Ehrhardt and Money's key findings – the high incidence of bisexuality or homosexuality among CAH girls. In a more recent study, only 5 per cent of a similar group of women reported bisexual or homosexual activity.[27]

97

One of the fundamental difficulties in interpreting any of these findings is that the behavioural observations came from parents and teachers who knew of the girls' abnormal physiological condition, and from the girls themselves. These supposedly objective descriptions could have been biased by their expectations. The children certainly did not have a normal childhood. Some did not have plastic surgery on their genitals until they were seven, and most had further vaginal surgery at adolescence.

The medicalisation of these children has probably had quite dramatic effects on their psychological development. Some hint of this comes from a study in 1984 by a Dutch researcher, Froukje Slijper.[28] She gave psychological tests designed to measure ideas of gender to CAH children and to a group of young diabetic patients. There was no difference between the two groups' results. Slijper argues that both had experienced chronic illness and hospitalisation, and both had rebelled against the intrusion of medical authority into their lives. She also suggests that these children were more aware of their situation and more insecure about themselves than the average child.

There is an even more fundamental source of bias underlying this research. Throughout this work there is the assumption that certain behaviours are intrinsically masculine or feminine – and so provide independent criteria for some 'biological' reality known as 'masculinity' or 'femininity'. This assumption ignores the evidence that these categories are social and cultural constructions that have changed historically as ideas about what is appropriate to each sex have altered. For instance, as the late Ruth Bleier, a neurobiologist at the University of Wisconsin at Madison, pointed out, this work accepts at face value 'the idea of tomboyism as an index of a characteristic called "masculinity", presumed to be as objective and innate a human feature as height and eye colour'.[29] As psychobiologist Richard Whalen of the University of California puts it: 'In the real world, both male and female rats always engage in vigorous outdoor activities. In our culture, we tend to characterise any person frequently engaging in vigorous outdoor activity as being masculine.'[30] Bleier has argued that the uncritical acceptance of these studies of 'gender role' in children with genetic disorders 'places the stamp of science on a set of unexamined social values and judgments concerning gender'.

Changing Sex the Natural Way

Another well-known study, open to similar critiques, forms part of the 'evidence' in this ongoing battle. Julianne Imperato-McGinley of Cornell University Medical School and her colleagues happened upon a remarkable genetic disorder.[31] In three rural villages in Santo Domingo they found children who were apparently girls until puberty, then switched sex: their voices deepened, facial hair sprouted, and they grew penises. Although they had been reared as girls, they happily adopted a masculine 'gender identity', married and fathered children.

This strange phenomenon is the result of a rare genetic mishap. These individuals are genetically male, with XY sex chromosomes, but lack a particular enzyme, 5-alpha-reductase, which is responsible for converting testosterone to an even more potent androgen known as DHT (dihydro-testosterone). Their internal male sex organs develop normally, but the lack of DHT means that their external genitalia are ambiguous or female-looking. But it is testosterone, which they produce normally, that is responsible for the development of masculine sexual characteristics at puberty, so when they reach the age of about twelve their 'maleness' suddenly emerges.

Imperato-McGinley interpreted the fact that these individuals are happy to become boys, despite a childhood spent as a girl, to mean that gender identity – an individual's sense of belonging to one sex or the other – must be caused by hormones at puberty. The surge of testosterone in the male adolescent, she argues, is responsible for his gender identity. Other researchers, such as LeVay, say that these individuals found being boys unproblematic because their brains were normally masculinised by testosterone in the womb, despite the fact that their external genitalia suffered from a lack of DHT.[32] He points out that this same disorder has turned up among the Simbari Anga people in the Eastern Highlands of Papua New Guinea, a culture radically different from that of the Dominican Republic; nonetheless, here too the 'girls' change into boys at puberty, 'albeit with much turmoil', says LeVay.[33]

Yet other commentators – Anne Fausto-Sterling for one – point out that the villagers in the Dominican Republic, at least, soon came to recognise which infants had this anomalous condition and even invented a name for them, which means 'penis at twelve': these individuals could not have been reared as 'normal' girls, and may even realise what is in store for them.[34] Even more significant, perhaps, is the observation that marked advantages accrue to males in both the cultures studied. Boys are more highly valued, and have much more freedom than girls do.

The Aftermath of a Medical Mistake

An 'experiment of medicine' has provided more fuel for controversy. Between 1940 and 1971 American doctors gave an oestrogenic drug, diethylstilbestrol (DES), to several million pregnant women in the mistaken belief that it would reduce their risk of miscarriage. This treatment made the exposed children much more likely to develop certain cancers of the reproductive tract. But what fascinated American psychiatrists most was whether the drugs had also altered the individuals' sexual behaviour. Studies on rats suggested that prenatal DES should act like androgens and 'masculinise' females.

In 1984 Heino Meyer-Bahlburg of the Psychiatric Institute in New York and Anke Ehrhardt compared thirty women whose mothers had taken DES with thirty women who were referred to the same clinic because they had abnormal cervical smears.[35] The researchers could find no difference in the 'psychosexual milestones' – events such as age at first boyfriend or first sexual intercourse. After further study of the same women, they concluded in 1989 that DES-exposed women show 'less orientation toward parenting' than the controls, although the differences were not statistically significant. When the women were asked whether they would prefer being a mother to having a career, 'most subjects in both groups wanted to have both'. Moreover, according to their mothers' reports, the DES-exposed women engaged in less, not more, rough-and-tumble play during childhood than the controls did.

The researchers could find 'no consistent group differences in other domains of gender-role behaviour'. They reported, however, that more of these DES-exposed women said they were lesbians or bisexual than did the controls. The fact that more of the control group were married Catholic women, while many of the DES women were unmarried students – and so likely to have more opportunity to form unconventional sexual relationships – did not seem to disturb the researchers' conviction that sexual orientation is probably influenced by prenatal hormones.

This highlights a persistent shortcoming of research in this field. What constitutes a genuine control group for a psychological or hormonal study of women who live with other women and have sexual relationships with them? Researchers often compare these women to their own wives, or to the wives of their friends or colleagues. 'It would be helpful', wrote leading sex researchers, as they attempted to pull together all the contradictory findings, 'if scientists employed double-blind designs and had control groups matched on a wide range of variables' – methodologies that are standard practice in most fields of research.[36] A cautionary tale of the potential pitfalls comes from Ehrhardt and Money's study of ten girls born with masculinised genitalia because their mothers had been given androgenic progestins during pregnancy to discourage miscarriage.[37] The researchers reported that the girls had higher IQs than the population at large, sparking off a flurry of research into the potential IQ-boosting effects of testosterone. But when scientists at last devised an appropriate control group – family members not exposed to the abnormal prenatal environment, for instance – the superior intellectual performance disappeared.

Psychobiologists have also searched for differences in perceptual abilities or problem-solving skills. They hope to find that females 'masculinised' in the womb will be better at mathematics and have a greater spatial ability than the average girl. Results have been 'mixed' and 'inconsistent'. Two studies failed to find any difference, two found that CAH females were worse than 'normal' girls; only one succeeded in recording enhanced performance by CAH girls on spatial tests. But researchers refuse to give up. Hampson and Kimura, for instance, conclude that the data are 'suggestive', and that overall the evidence indicates that 'sex hormones can exert lasting effects on the neural template'.[38]

Boys exposed to DES *in utero* have also come under scientific scrutiny, but again, the findings refused to fit neatly into gender stereotypes. Some studies suggest that the boys were 'feminised' – because they were more interested in 'social service and writing' than the boys assigned to the control group were. However, DES boys were also apparently keen on mathematics, which is regarded as a masculine trait. Boys exposed to DES were also said to be 'demasculinised' because they were less interested in actively participating in sport than those in the control group. Yet the DES group were simultaneously considered to be 'masculinised' with regard to 'passive viewing of sport', because a number of the youngsters interviewed liked watching competitive contest sports.[39]

This line of argument may yet resurface in another arena – the growing debate about oestrogens in the environment. It now seems incontrovertible that certain foods and a range of synthetic chemicals mimic human oestrogens. Two researchers, Richard Sharpe of the MRC's Reproductive Biology Unit in Edinburgh and Niels Skakkebaek of the University of Copenhagen, have blamed such 'environmental oestrogens' for the rise in the rate of testicular cancer and various malformations of the penis and testicles, as well as an apparent fall in average sperm counts over the past 50 years. Sharpe suggests that the recent rise in the incidence of other cancers, such as breast cancer in women, could have similar origins. All these abnormalities could have become more common as a result of the increased exposure of fetuses to oestrogens – creating a parallel to the DES medical disaster.[40]

No one knows yet whether environmental oestrogens are responsible for the rise in reproductive cancers. But the possibility is a researcher's nightmare. There are many potential culprits: pesticides, PCBs, car exhaust emissions and even the breakdown products of common industrial detergents or contraceptive pills in drinking water could act as weak oestrogens, as could a shift to high-fat, low fibre diets, or particular foods such as milk and soya bean products. Unlike their colleagues in psychoneuroendocrinology, however, most of the scientists working in this field are cautious about extrapolating from their meagre data. They are reluctant, for instance, to suggest that this environmental 'sea of oestrogens' might have led to an increase in the incidence of homosexuality in modern times. When questioned by me on this theme, three leading researchers in the field refused to be drawn; they responded: 'I don't think oestrogens would have that effect', 'That is a provocative claim for which there is no evidence' and 'That is outside my area of expertise'.[41] Human sexuality, they pointed out, is not notably constrained by hormones.

The Shaky Foundations of Sex

Everyone is either male or female – that seems to be firmly grounded in the biology of our species. Yet there is no necessary connection between chromosomal sex, hormones, gonads or genitalia – let alone behaviour. Gender is not mandated by biology.

Incontrovertible physical evidence for this surprising conclusion comes from rare cases of individuals born with ambiguous genitals. These so-called 'intersex' individuals are generally referred to specialist clinics, where clinicians decide to which gender to assign the child. They do this not by discovering the 'true' sex, as this has no fixed meaning. Rather, they examine the genitalia and decide whether plastic surgery can most readily transform them into a plausible penis or a vagina. Unless the infant has a 'good-sized' penis amenable to augmentations, the baby is declared a female. Intersex individuals tend to be raised as girls, as it is considered easier to create a 'good-enough' vagina.

These clinicians acknowledge the pragmatic grounds on which they assign gender to a child. Yet in what they believe to be their patients' best interests, they perpetuate the belief that gender consists of two mutually exclusive types.[42] They stress that the parents must be led to believe that the 'true sex' of their child has been discovered. In reality, the doctors merely provide the right genitals to go along with the subsequent socialisation that will establish gender. Parents are advised to tell friends that the baby was mistakenly assumed to be a male at first because there was 'an excess of skin on the clitoris'. To still any rumours, the parents can exhibit the baby's reconstructed genitalia to friends and relatives.

A parallel, though very different, debate surrounds the 'sex testing' of women Olympic athletes. Instigated in 1968 at the height of the athletics 'cold war', ostensibly to stop men masquerading as women, it coincided with anxiety about the increasingly masculine appearance of women athletes. The sex tests began as physical gynaecological examinations. When athletes complained of the humiliation, the sports officials turned to a chromosomal test, judging it to be both more discreet and more authoritative. Yet this move led to the exclusion from competition of top athletes who were clearly female but had some genetic anomaly. In 1992 the Olympic Committee persisted with its policy, introducing an even more sophisticated test for a single gene, recently claimed to be the 'male determining factor'. Meanwhile, leading medical geneticists and sports doctors said the tests unfairly excluded some women from sport.[43]

Only Two Genders?

The scientific pursuit of biological origins for gender difference presupposes a tidy sexual divide: a dualism or dimorphism that separates men and women into distinctly different sorts of beings. Early sexologists who bravely acknowledged their homosexuality argued for a third category.[44] The German Heinrich Ulrichs described a third sex, which he called urnings, that would include homosexuals and bisexuals, among others. His fellow countryman Magnus Hirschfield argued for sexual 'intermediaries', to include homosexuals and trans-vestites.

But these classificatory schemes did little to enhance the status or establish the normality of sexual 'deviants'. In the scientific model, there are only two 'natural' kinds of indivi-dual, as Helen Longino, a philosopher of science at Rice University in Houston, Texas, explains: 'one with female repro-ductive capacity, feminine behaviour and a sexuality oriented towards men, the other with male reproductive capacity, mas-culine behaviour, and a sexuality oriented towards women.'[45] Sexuality and social identity must be tied to one of two pos-sible reproductive roles. In the 'normal' case, all the female parts – genes, brains, genitalia, gender-typical ways of be-having – are united in one body, and all the male parts in another body.

But things sometimes go wrong, the story goes. Genitally male or female individuals can end up with a brain of the wrong 'sex'. As a result, they may have the wrong sexual orientation, and be attracted to people of the same sex. Or they may have the wrong 'gender-role behaviour'. A woman may be more interested in being an engineer or a stockbroker than a wife and mother. Even the way an individual thinks and reasons may go awry – a woman could end up with the cog-nitive abilities meant for the male sex, for instance, and so excel at mathematics or architecture instead of English and foreign languages. Thus the scientists argue.

All these characteristics are purported to be imprinted in our brains before birth, depending on whether we were exposed to a particular hormone. People deviate from any of these norms if various parts have been mixed inappropriately, through some developmental mishap, and they may need medical help to right the mix. 'It's like an auto parts store,' Longino writes. 'Proper management of the inventory means that the right parts will reach their destinations. Carelessness means that a part for the diesel model will be installed in the gasoline-powered model and vice versa, with eventual dys-function.'

Longino and other feminist scholars, notably Lynda Birke,

have argued that it is possible to think, instead, of a multiplicity of genders.[46] Nothing compels us to conclude that there are only two ways of being human, with 'mix-and-match' variations seen as deviations from the standard pattern. As the slogan now appearing on the T-shirts of American gay men opposed to the ban on homosexuals in the military says: 'You don't have to sleep with a woman to fight like a man'.[47]

Our everyday experience of ourselves and other people constantly reaffirms the common observation that individual personalities, enthusiasms and capabilities do not come tied up in neat pink or blue packages. Only with enormous difficulty can 'brain sex' be considered a unitary concept. In the latest rearguard action to try to rescue the beleaguered hormones-in-the-womb-sex-your-brain theory, Sandra Witelson of McMaster University in Hamilton, Ontario, acknowledges that 'brain sex' can be multifaceted – regions of the brain can become 'male' or 'female' independently of each other.[48] The result, she argues, is a mosaic of sexes dotted around the brain – a 'neural sexual mosaicism'. Her account purports to explain why it is possible for a woman to excel at mathematics and physics yet be a devoted mother, or why a man might work on a construction site but study foreign languages in his spare time. Those are my examples; Witelson's example is more bizarre. She argues that 'neural sexual mosaicism' means that it makes sense to talk of a 'male lesbian' – a man who looks male, acts like a man, is heterosexual, but has some 'female-type mental characteristics'.

Witelson presents no mechanism, and no data, to substantiate her model. Its mere plausibility in the face of our knowledge of human diversity is meant to count as evidence. Yet her account takes our experience of human beings as varied, diverse and changeable and then gives it back to us, transformed into some apparently unalterable inner essence – some hypothetical brain programming in the womb.

Gay Hormones, Gay Brains, Gay Genes

Our cultural preoccupations seem eerily to echo the concerns of the closing years of the past century – so argues the American historian Elaine Showalter in *Sexual Anarchy*.[49] According to Showalter, Victorian *fin-de-siècle* literature and art, medicine and science were similarly concerned with the attempt to understand sexual difference – to pinpoint the essence of man and woman, and to diagnose and define the sexual 'ambiguity' or 'deviance' embodied in hermaphrodites or homosexuals. The science of sex hormones, behaviour and the brain was born then. Today, its descendants claim to be able to trace the origins of human homosexuality to the hormonal milieu in the womb.

Ever since the sex hormones were first discovered, scientists have searched for evidence that homosexuals are a sort of hormonal intersex. Acting on this cultural stereotype, early researchers in the field were confident that homosexual men would turn out to have a distinctive ratio of sex hormones, intermediate between heterosexual men and women. Their project ultimately failed, but not without a struggle. Researchers worked hard to explain their 'anomalous' findings so that they could salvage their theory. When they came across heterosexual men with relatively low androgen levels, for instance, these men were deemed to be 'latent homosexuals'.[50]

Today, most scientists acknowledge, as John Bancroft puts it, that 'most of these studies have been notable for their naivety and for the almost total lack of control of the many variables that can influence isolated hormone levels.'[51] Clinicians now agree that men who develop low testosterone levels through accident or illness, for example, do not suddenly become gay, and that injections of testosterone do not cause homosexual men to prefer women as their sexual partners.

The physical stereotypes fail at every level. Earlier claims that homosexual men have a more feminine physique than heterosexual men also suffered from faulty sampling,

107

according to Bancroft. The supposedly weedy gay men examined by scientists in the 1950s were all psychiatric patients; other 'neurotic' men in mental hospitals of the day turned out to be similarly androgynous in build. No anatomical or endocrine pattern distinguishes male homosexuals from heterosexuals, Bancroft concludes.

Similar failings beset studies of lesbians over the past thirty years. One study claimed that lesbians were taller than heterosexual women. Another said they were not taller, but had bigger breasts and thicker waists.[52] The latest attempt to find a hormonal difference between lesbians and heterosexual women has also proved a dismal failure. In 1987 Anke Ehrhardt and her colleagues looked for differences in blood levels of testosterone, androstenedione and cortisol in the two groups of women, but could find nothing distinctive about the lesbians.[53] Nor were there any significant differences in sexual behaviour, apart from the obvious one.

Hormonal Test for Homosexuality?

A rather more complicated hormonal definition of homosexuality has also failed to live up to its early promise. Günter Dörner, director of the Institute of Experimental Endocrinology at Humboldt University in Berlin, has long argued that hormones produced by the pituitary gland in the brain can be used as a marker to determine whether someone's brain has been made 'masculine' or 'feminine', thanks to its prenatal hormonal environment.[54] Dörner claims that the presence or absence of a surge in luteinizing hormone (LH) from the pituitary after an injection of oestrogen reveals the 'sex' of the brain. He maintains that male-to-female transsexuals – men who think of themselves as women – and homosexual men show an LH surge and thus have prenatally determined female brains, whereas lesbians and female-to-male transsexuals have a male pattern of LH secretion.

Louis Gooren of the Free University Hospital in Amsterdam is critical of Dörner's theory. In a study replicating the conditions of Dörner's work, Gooren and his colleagues were unable to find a significant difference between the hormones of homosexual and heterosexual men. Some heterosexuals, as well as some homosexuals, showed a supposedly female-like response. And in another series of studies, Gooren has shown that this supposedly permanent feature of the central nervous system is remarkably changeable.[55] He found that male-to-female transsexuals do not show an LH surge before treatment. Yet after a sex change operation, which involves castration and treatment with oestrogen, the same individuals develop an LH surge. This proves, he says, that in humans the presence or absence of an LH surge 'is not definitively and irrevocably designated' before or just after birth. In men, it is not the central nervous system but probably something secreted by their testicles that prohibits an LH surge in some individuals, he suspects, and this could vary according to age, body weight, exposure to viral infections and the use of cannabis or alcohol, as well as habitual levels of exercise and psychological stress. All these factors have to be taken into account in comparing the testicular function of two groups of men. Gooren's subjects may well have been less distinctly different than Dörner's apparently were because, gay or straight, they were all hospital workers or their friends. 'Other recruiting methods may result in greater differences,' which are then mistakenly attributed to their sexual orientation rather than their life circumstances.

Dörner is perhaps most famous for his claim that he has produced homosexual rodents that mimic human homosexuality. He believes that he can turn 'straight' male rats gay in the womb by stressing their mothers during pregnancy.[56] A typical regimen involves confining the pregnant rat in a Plexiglas tube under bright lights, for forty-five minutes three times a day, during the last week of pregnancy. Anyone who knows anything about rats knows that they find this treatment very stressful indeed – after unescapable, unpredictable electric shock, closely confining a rat is just about the worst thing you can do to it.[57] Neurobiologist Simon LeVay argues that this sort of research shows that the stress 'does not have to be very extreme or prolonged' to have effects on the rat fetuses – with the implication that it could easily happen in ordinary human pregnancies too.[58]

109

Inadvertently, however, Dörner and his colleagues have themselves helped to make clear the absurdity of animal models of homosexuality. They typically judge the 'sexual orientation' of their rats by placing a hormonally manipulated one with a non-manipulated one of the same sex, and charting their sexual interaction. In one experiment Dörner caged supposedly demasculinised male rats – the putative gay ones – with androgenised, aroused female rats – prototype lesbians in his book. The 'homosexual' females mounted the 'homosexual' males, with the result that each animal managed to behave both heterosexually (according to object choice) and homosexually (by the criterion of mating behaviour) at exactly the same moment.[59]

Not all scientists have leapt from rats to humans with such verve. A trio of American psychobiologists, Richard Whalen and his colleagues, recently tried to distance themselves from Dörner's work with the following example.[60] Rat researchers acknowledge that Swedish male laboratory rats readily show lordosis, even without hormonal treatments, while American rats of the Sprague-Dawley strain rarely do, whatever the hormonal provocation. Nonetheless, neither American nor Swedish researchers 'consider that the Swedish rats are homosexual', Whalen and his colleagues point out.

Yet researchers continue to search for new animal models of homosexuality. Angela Pattatucci and Dean Hamer at the prestigious National Cancer Institute in Bethesda, Maryland, are studying a mutant fruit fly which they think looks promising.[61] The flies produce functional sperm, but they do not mount and inseminate females; according to the researchers, this makes them behaviourally infertile. Even better would be a rat with mutant genes and a propensity to mount other rats of its sex. 'No one has found a good rodent model of genetically based homosexuality,' reports the newsletter of the National Institutes of Health. 'We'd love to have such an animal,' says Hamer. A voice of sanity comes from Eva Eicher of Jackson Laboratories in Bar Harbor, Maine, who points out that 'it would be very difficult to recognize hereditary homosexuality in animals'.

Anatomy Lesson from AIDS Victims' Brains

As the animal research continues, the idea that some people are born with a hormonally imprinted gay brain refuses to go away. It gained a new lease of life and the imprimatur of science in 1991, thanks to a paper published in America's leading scientific journal, *Science*.[62] The world's media eagerly reported a discovery so arcane that, had it not involved gay men, it would have been roundly ignored. The excitement centred on a tiny cluster of cells, about a tenth of a cubic millimetre in volume, known as the third interstitial nucleus of the anterior hypothalamus, or INAH 3. Earlier research had suggested that this region is fractionally bigger in men than in women. What hit the headlines was Simon LeVay's announcement that this part of the brain is bigger in heterosexual men than in homosexual ones. He had no evidence about how this difference, should it come to be regarded as real, might have arisen. Nonetheless, he said that his finding suggests that 'sexual orientation has a biological substrate'.

LeVay thinks that gays are born, not made. He believes that sexual orientation is established in the womb, by the hormones to which the fetus is exposed. His work on the anatomy of the brain is just the beginning: the next step is to identify the genes that influence sexual orientation. LeVay's conclusions rest on several assumptions. First, he speculates that his cluster of cells controls 'masculine' sexuality in males. The evidence for this is that if scientists destroy a rat's hypothalamus, it no longer mates. LeVay's second assumption is grounded on work by Laura Allen and Roger Gorski and their colleagues at the University of California Medical School at Los Angeles, who had previously found INAH 3 to be larger in men than in women.[63] From this, LeVay jumps to the conclusion that this region of the brain 'could be involved in the generation of male-typical sexual behaviour'. He decides that INAH 3 makes men sexually interested in women, specifically. According to LeVay, lesbians and heterosexual men should have large INAH 3s, and heterosexual women and gay men should have small ones.

Brains from lesbians were not readily to hand, but deaths

from AIDS provided LeVay with a supply of gay brains for analysis. His data rest on the autopsy of the brains of nineteen gay men, sixteen presumed heterosexual men and six presumed heterosexual women. From this, LeVay concluded that, on average, gay men have INAH 3s that are half the size of heterosexual men's.

The popular press widely reported LeVay's work, accepting it at face value. But measuring the size of tiny, ill-defined regions of the brain is not easy. As John Maddox, editor of the British science journal *Nature*, pointed out in an article entitled 'Is Homosexuality Hard-Wired?', 'LeVay makes the technique sound much simpler than it is.'[64] Dick Swaab, a leading researcher in this field, also seems sceptical of LeVay's results. Swaab says he has not measured LeVay's region in the brains he has studied, because he has found no good markers for the region.[65] What LeVay measured is not a concrete structure with definable limits. The nucleus is composed of cells similar to those outside it, and the boundary is unclear.

But there are problems even if the data are taken at face value. The range of measurements recorded in the nineteen gay men is huge – spanning a twentyfold difference. Some gay men had nuclei as large as those of the sixteen heterosexual men, 'which in itself shows that the third nucleus is not an unambiguous determinant of sexual orientation', Maddox writes. 'The scatter of the measured sizes suggest that nuclear size, if in any sense a "cause", is neither a unique nor an unambiguous determinant of homosexual behaviour,' he concludes.

In fact, LeVay's was not the first report of an anatomical difference between the brains of homosexual and heterosexual men. Swaab and his colleagues in Amsterdam won that distinction in 1990, when they reported that a part of the brain which influences circadian rhythms, the suprachiasmatic nucleus, is twice as large in gay men as in heterosexual men.[66] Soon after LeVay's paper was published, Laura Allen and Roger Gorski claimed that a bundle of nerve cells connecting the left and right sides of the brain, the anterior commissure, is larger on average in gay men than in heterosexuals.[67] These discoveries have inspired less media excitement, presumably because they are even more tenuously connected with sexual behaviour, and so few people see them as serious candidates for the biological cause of homosexuality.

There is yet another problem with LeVay's research, highlighted by Anne Fausto-Sterling: the fact that he knew virtually nothing about the sexual behaviour of the men in his study, apart from the statement that some were gay. It is conceivable, for instance, that the brain differences he found, if they are confirmed, are linked with the frequency of sexual activity rather than with sexual orientation *per se*, Fausto-Sterling argues.[68] Again, no one has any idea about the direction of causality. Any differences in brain anatomy could be the result, rather than the cause, of different lifestyles.

Born, Not Made? The Ideologies of Gender

LeVay – who is himself gay, and has helped to found a new organisation in Los Angeles, the West Hollywood Institute for Gay and Lesbian Education – welcomes the idea that brains are made gay in the womb through the action of hormones. But LeVay is a self-confessed newcomer to sex research; he made his name for his work on the brain mechanisms underlying visual perception. He says he feels he was born gay, 'though rationally I have to say that [my conviction] doesn't prove it', he told a journalist from *Science*.[69] He was inspired to look for sex in the brain when his lover died of AIDS. 'I felt if I didn't find anything, I would give up a scientific career altogether,' he told *Newsweek*.[70] In his book *The Sexual Brain*, LeVay acknowledges that, as a newcomer, he has a 'certain innocent enthusiasm' for neuroanatomical studies of sex.[71] Candidly, he describes his position: 'In any field of study, one eventually gets weighed down, paralysed even, by the sheer mass of conflicting findings and theories. I have not yet reached that point.' His book shows all the missionary zeal of a new convert.

LeVay is convinced that if the hormones-in-the-womb-make-you-gay theory gains wide acceptance, it will be impossible for anyone to argue that homosexuality is either curable, or freely chosen and sinful. The danger, he acknowledges, is that homosexuality will be seen as a defect that can be prevented by prenatal diagnosis and abortion, or 'fixed' by hormonal treatments.[72] We have been here before, it seems.

Before the 1970s, psychiatrists regarded homosexuality as a mental disorder, and devised many ingenious treatments – ranging from hormone injections to electric shocks linked to photos of nude men – to 'cure' their patients. Some homosexuals fought back by arguing that their sexuality was fixed, and therefore not amenable to change; at the very least, homosexuals deserved pity and tolerance, not aversion therapy or drugs. In Radclyffe Hall's famous lesbian novel *The Well of Loneliness*, the heroine, Stephen, is a tragic 'invert', condemned by birth to wear men's suits, go hunting and fishing, and lust after women.

The limitations of this line of defence have been painfully clear for decades. Why do some gays and lesbians today still find these explanations so powerful? LeVay, who says he spent his English childhood with a father who was hostile to him because he was not 'masculine' enough, seems to seek solace in nature; he concludes his book by arguing that our sexuality is limited and constrained by our biology: 'Like waterlilies, we swing to and fro with the currents of life, yet our roots moor us each to our own spot on the river's floor.'

Gay Genes Are 'Natural'

Nature has always proved enormously alluring – as if the taunts and humiliations emanating from the heterosexual world can be neutralised once and for all by an appeal to our species' evolutionary past. Biologists who are in sympathy with the gay movement often seem to believe that if they could find a gene for gayness, everyone would have to acknowledge that the persistance of homosexuality through the millennia must indicate that the 'gay' gene carries some evolutionary advantage. Such researchers argue that homosexuality, built into brain architecture, is not a defect, but 'a way of increasing the diversity of temperaments and behaviours available to our species'. Ergo, homosexuality is just as 'natural' as heterosexuality.[73]

114

Richard Pillard of Boston University School of Medicine, acknowledged to be the first outwardly gay psychiatrist in the USA, is drawn to these explanations, and claims to have found evidence that gay genes exist. Recently, Pillard and his colleague, Michael Bailey of Northwestern University, interviewed fifty-six pairs of identical made twins and 54 pairs of fraternal twins.[74] They report that if one identical twin is gay, the other is almost three times more likely to be gay than if the twins are fraternal. Their finding, coming on the heels of LeVay's announcement, was widely reported in the press as 'more evidence' that gays are born, not made. With Yvonne Agyei, Bailey and Pillard have recently reported that among identical girl twins they studied, both were lesbians in almost half of the pairs, while only 16 per cent of the non-identical twin sisters were lesbians.[75]

Yet these studies do not demonstrate that shared genes made the twins gay: twins are likely to have shared similar experiences in childhood, too. Even to begin to tease apart nature and nurture, researchers would have to compare twins raised separately. The genetic theory also fails to explain why only one of many pairs of identical twins in the study was gay. Most of the discordant identical twins scored at opposite ends of the 'Kinsey scale' which ranks individuals according to their sexual behaviour on a seven-point scale ranging from strictly homosexual to exclusively heterosexual.

Nonetheless, some gay campaigners have already warmly embraced these recent studies. These findings reduce being gay 'to something like being left-handed, which is in fact all that it is', says Randy Shilts, a gay journalist based in San Francisco.[76] Homosexuality is innate, a spokesman for the Campaign for Homosexual Equality recently told *Living* magazine, so it can no longer be seen as 'a perverted choice'.[77] 'Doubts have been expressed about whether genetic engineering might be used to screen out homosexuality,' the spokesman said, 'but my view is this isn't a threat in the foreseeable future.'

Don't Worry – It May Never Happen

The history of the medical management of homosexuality, or of women's supposed internal complaints, militates against such complacency. 'Cures' have invariably soon followed the diagnosis, and the fact that they did not work discouraged no one. As one commentator put it, 'The efficacy of the treatment has rarely been the criterion governing its use.'[78] In search of cures, one clinician castrated homosexual men and transplanted testicular tissue from heterosexual men. Apparently at least eleven men underwent this operation between 1916 and 1921, albeit with little success.[79] In the 1960s another clinician devised a new surgical technique to cure homosexuality, this time centred on the brain. Some seventy-five men deemed sexually abnormal – mostly incarcerated in prisons or mental institutions – had part of their brain, the hypothalamus, removed. The practice ended when sex researchers in Germany banded together to demand a moratorium on this form of psychosurgery.[80] Most recently, Günter Dörner has suggested that pregnant women might have hormone injections to guard against the risk of having homosexual offspring. He also claims to have cured homosexual rats with injections of the drug lisuride.[81]

American sexologists at the research institute founded by Kinsey offer us the vision of a brave new world of research on pregnant women.[82] They suggest that the amniotic fluid removed from a woman having her fetus checked for Down's syndrome could also be tested for its testosterone content. Researchers could then check up on these children some years later to see which had become homosexual. Armed with this information, doctors could begin to offer routine hormone tests in normal pregnancies. June Reinisch and her colleagues seem to welcome the prospect of such prenatal counselling and 'therapeutic' interventions.

It is not only homosexuals who are at risk from the growing ascendancy of biological explanations for sexual difference. Women of all sexual persuasions have much to fear from the notion that femininity, or the perceived lack of it, is determined before birth. Such a theoretical framework can help to

116

create a cultural climate that seriously damages women's prospects of winning equal rights in education and the workplace. Already, researchers such as Kimura have concluded that women will probably never feature strongly in engineering or physics, because their brains just can't cope with the requisite spatial tasks. Women, however, swell the ranks of workers in medical diagnostics – presumably as poorly paid technicians in radiography and ultrasonography – 'where perceptual skills are important'.[83]

Only a direct examination of the cultural preconceptions surrounding gender difference and sexual difference can begin to bring this debate out of the shadows of scientific expertise and into the public arena. There is a pressing need to account for the current resurgence of biological explanations of sexual difference, be it a matter of 'gender role' or 'sexual orientation'. Here, I shall concentrate on homosexuality, but many of the same arguments apply to issues surrounding gender. In fact, the status of women is intimately linked to attitudes to homosexuals, because both feminism and gay liberation threaten traditional gender roles. Homosexuality, as Anne Fausto-Sterling puts it, 'is part of the sex–gender political system' in so far as fear of homosexuality helps to enforce heterosexual gender roles.[84] Traditionalists invoke gays and lesbians as awful warnings of the dire consequences of deviation from gender stereotypes.

The scientific community, in turn, picks up these cultural ideas and plays them back to us, now vested with scientific authority, as facts of nature. They search for parts of the brain that apparently differ in men and women as evidence that the sexes are born different, and inevitably must behave differently. They expect gay men to be physiologically like women (because only women are meant to be sexually attracted to men), and lesbians to be like men, and so re-present the sought-after male/female divide in another set of brains. 'Thus the political struggle about gay civil rights and gay acceptance inevitably becomes part of a power struggle about gender. It is this that fuels the frenzied concern about the causes of homosexuality,' Fausto-Sterling argues.

117

In 1973 gay activists won a great victory: the American Psychiatric Association voted (albeit with much internal dissension) that homosexuality was not, after all, a mental disorder. But this breakthrough, riding on the wave of the human rights movements of the 1960s, did nothing to discourage biomedical researchers from seeking a physical cause for homosexuality. The pathology most probably lay in some neuroendocrine abnormality, the scientists argued.[85]

Essentialism Rides Again

One would like to think that the best counter to this neo-essentialism – the notion that explanations for the way people are lie in some inner essence that is biologically programmed or inexorably fixed in the first few years of life, as the Freudians would have it – is simply to recount the wealth of social and cultural evidence against such an interpretation. Many social psychologists and sociologists have stalwartly taken this line of attack. They have described studies indicating that all manner of people, of different ages, class, race, education and employment, fall in love with someone of the same sex, and that an individual's sexual 'identity' may shift dramatically over their life course. The labels 'gay', 'bisexual' and 'lesbian' are recent inventions – a century or two ago, people talked only of homosexual acts, and condemned or condoned the behaviour, but did not regard such sexual acts as indicating anything about a person's sexual essence or identity. Today these labels are best viewed as political statements or as attempts to forge some identity as a beleaguered minority, not as indicators of some true biological essence. 'There is little evidence that these persons share a common biography, that they recognise their true identities, or that they have common psychological profiles as measured through standard psychological inventories,' writes John Gagnon, professor of sociology and psychology at the State University of New York at Stony Brook.[86]

Why isn't this diversity more widely acknowledged? Part of the problem is that the very phenomenon is inevitably in flux. The present diversity of people who consider themselves homosexual is largely the consequence of the ideology of egalitarianism current in the United States and Europe by the late 1960s, and is constantly changing, as shifts in thinking and conduct take place within the culture. Scientific ideas form a central part of this cultural process, influencing and being influenced by their larger social context. Thus Gagnon argues that 'the pre-1950s essentialist theories influenced the thinking of "homosexuals" about who they were and indirectly sustained the repressive machinery and attitudes of the larger society towards the "homosexual"'. In the 1950s, many lesbians, for instance, were trapped in 'butch' and 'fem' roles, believing that a person had to be either masculine or feminine – in essentialist thought, there are only two rigidly stereotypical ways of being human. In an ironic dialectical twist, the lesbians' role-playing was then cited as further evidence of the biological inevitability of these categories.

In the anti-feminist and anti-gay backlash of the 1980s and 1990s – fuelled in part by the AIDS epidemic but also reflecting the blossoming of repressive ideologies throughout much of the West – the gay community is again being fed essentialist explanations, and is once again in danger of beginning to make them seem true. The New Right has been primarily concerned to advance biological explanations for social inequality, to justify the inevitability of poverty and racial and sexual discrimination on the grounds that the socially disadvantaged are innately inferior. In this climate, homosexuality is inevitably also seen as 'in the hormones' or, more recently, 'in the genes'.

Is Homosexuality A Choice?

In this context, the gay liberationists and lesbian feminists who have long argued that homosexuality is a 'choice' are in for a hard time. In the increasingly individualised and conservative cultures of North America and Europe, 'choice' has become a problematic notion. If gayness is a choice, it risks being seen as a frivolous one – an escape from the responsibilities of the nuclear family. If it is a matter for individuals to choose freely, they must 'take responsibility' for their choice ('just say no') and face the consequences, just as the impoverished youth who turns to crime must face the short, sharp shock of some detention centre. A powerfully reiterated argument is: 'Society doesn't have to approve, or grant equal rights, to those who choose to behave in that way' – nor should others be encouraged to follow suit. If homosexuality is freely chosen by some individuals, a climate of tolerance will only encourage more citizens to deviate from the straight and narrow – so justifying political interventions such as 'Section 28' of the recent Local Government Act, which banned local councils in Britain from doing anything to 'promote' homosexuality. Children's books showing positive images of lesbian or gay parents were removed from most school libraries and classrooms. The veteran sex researcher John Money, who does not believe that homosexuals can choose their sexual preference, agrees that the idea is dangerous: 'Then they can be legally forced, under threat of punishment, to choose to be heterosexual.'[87]

So we arrive at the political climate of the 1990s, with many gay biologists and psychologists, as well as heterosexual ones, claiming that homosexuality is a matter of inner chemistry and brain wiring. Human sexuality is not like wet clay, they argue, but rather resembles pots that have been too long in the kiln – brittle, immutable, no longer open to change.[88]

There is a real danger of self-fulfilling prophecy here. Because essentialist ideas hold sway, individuals come to experience their own sexuality as categorical, as channelled towards one gender or another, and to think of their sexual lives as determined by inner forces. A good example comes from the cover story *Newsweek* ran in early 1992 (the cover showed a close-up of a baby's face, with the cover line: 'Is This Child Gay?'). The *Newsweek* story begins:

Until the age of 28, Doug Barnett (not his real name) was a practicing heterosexual. He was vaguely attracted to men, but with nurturing parents, a lively interest in sports and appropriate relations with women, he had little reason to question his proclivities. Then an astonishing thing happened: his identical twin brother 'came out' to him, revealing he was gay. Barnett, who believed sexual orientation is genetic, was bewildered. He recalls thinking, 'If this is inherited and we're identical twins – what's going on here?' To find out, he thought he should try sex with men. When he did, he says, 'The bells went off, for the first time. Those homosexual encounters were more fulfilling.' A year later both twins told their parents they were gay.[89]

But such experiences are far from proof that human beings do in fact have a core sexual orientation. Cross-cultural studies have cast doubt on this view; anthropologists have discovered enormous diversity in sexual systems in other cultures.[90] Even within our own culture, sex is not so simple, and the central danger of the essentialist view – as two American sociologists, Philip Blumstein and Pepper Schwartz, argue – is that it ignores the ways in which sexuality emerges in the context of a relationship, and is intimately tied up with the processes that lead to the creation of a sense of self.[91] 'Sexuality has been perceived as emanating from a core or innate *desire* that directs an individual's sex life,' they write. But they see desire as emerging from a cultural context, from 'the circumstances and meanings available to individuals; it is a product of socialisation, opportunity and interpretation'. To explain homosexuality, they argue, we should not turn to biology but, rather, consider 'the gender roles currently available and the societal organisation of opportunities'.

Yet male sexuality in our culture is shaped by the belief that men have a sometimes overpowering sex drive, creating sexual needs that cannot be repressed. This may help to explain why gay men, more than lesbians, seem drawn towards essentialist explanations. It is possible that men as a rule are actually more alienated from the context of their own sexuality than women tend to be. Men may be more likely to experience themselves as driven by internal biology, as a result of growing up in a culture which tells them that male sexuality is like that. They may then experience their bodies as having strong sexual urges, emanating from some inner biological core, and triggered not by relationship but by a physical image, a particular look, a contemporary style.

In Western culture, women's sexuality is organised by other than physical cues. A premium is placed on relational aspects, and deep friendship, admiration and companionship become the wellsprings of erotic attachment and response. As Sandra Bem, a psychologist at Cornell University well known for her work on psychological tests probing masculinity and femininity, describes herself:

> Although some of the (very few) individuals to whom I have been attracted during my 47 years have been men and some have been women, what those individuals have in common has nothing to do with either their biological sex or mine – from which I conclude not that I am attracted to both sexes, but that my sexuality is organised around dimensions other than sex.[92]

As a general rule, women may be more likely than men to see the inadequacies of a biological model which not only denies this social context, but seeks to identify chemical triggers for sexuality.

There is another possible source for the gender gap. By and large, men have less need than women do to contest existing gender roles. Indeed, it may not always be in their interests to do so. Women who call themselves lesbian feminists may in particular have come to relationships with other women as part of their dissatisfaction with, and rebellion against, traditional female gender roles. For them, lesbianism is explicitly part of a campaign to resist being assigned an inferior social role on grounds of biological sex. Gay men, as men, still have access to many of the benefits accruing to their gender in virtually every modern culture.[93]

I have tried to explore some of the sociocultural forces underlying the current fascination with biological accounts that attempt to explain why men and women apparently behave differently in various ways, and why some have sexual encounters with partners of the same sex while others do not. It is important to stress the complexity of the interactions between scientific ideas and public conceptions of these issues, and to emphasise the ways in which both feminists and the gay community have resisted becoming 'objects' of scientific enquiry. One trivial example makes the point. In his lectures to other scientists, Dick Swaab, the neuroscientist who first claimed to find a difference between straight and gay brains, shows slides of the media response to his research. One slide gets a big laugh; it shows a classified ad from a Dutch gay magazine, which translated means, roughly: 'Nice guy with large hypothalamus seeks similar with enlarged suprachiasmatic nucleus'.[94] The meaning of these scientific 'facts' remains open to negotiation.

Yet what is so dangerous about these biological models for complex human phenomena is not just that they might lead to unfortunate consequences for homosexuals – though a medical campaign centred round a prenatal 'search and destroy' mission would no doubt carry in its wake an intensification of discrimination against gays and lesbians. What is even more frightening is that these simplistic biological explanations take sexuality, and the experience of being in a heterosexual or a homosexual relationship, out of its lived context. The tragedy is that these ideas, as they filter into our consciousness, may make us more likely to behave as if we really were sexually driven automatons – intent not on relationship but on mere physical couplings, genital *frisson*, with the sex object of our choice.

5

TIME FOR HORMONES?

MEDICAL MODELS OF MENOPAUSE

The widespread acceptance of hormone replacement therapy in the United States in the 1960s was largely due to the promotional efforts of a prominent Brooklyn gynaecologist, Robert Wilson. Oestrogen was originally given to menopausal women to reduce hot flushes and sweats, the short-term symptoms associated with the decline of natural oestrogen levels. But Wilson claimed much more for the treatment. In his polemic *Feminine Forever*, published in 1966, he called menopause a hormone 'deficiency disease' and listed twenty-six symptoms – including absent-mindedness, irritability, depression, frigidity, alcoholism and even suicide – that the 'youth pill' could avert.[1]

In 1963 he established the Wilson Foundation in New York to promote oestrogens, supported by $1.3 million in grants from the drug industry.[2] In that year he wrote in a medical journal: 'The unpalatable truth must be faced that all post-menopausal women are castrates.'[3] Nine years later he claimed:

Estrogen deficiency is as much a disease as thyroid, pancreatic or adrenal deficiency. No attempt will be made here to detail all of the unwholesome effects of this deficiency disease; a few will suffice, e.g. thinning of bones, dowager's hump, ugly body contours, flaccidity of the breast, and atrophy of the genitalia ... The estrogenic treatment of older women will inhibit oesteoporosis and thus help to prevent fractures, as long as they continue healthful activities and appropriate diets. Breasts and genital organs will not shrivel. Such women will be much more pleasant to live with and will not become dull and unattractive.[4]

Wilson's language makes it clear that rather more than a woman's health is at stake here; women's continued attractiveness and sexual availability are high on the agenda. Even in contemporary accounts, beneath all the beneficial claims for hormone replacement therapy lies the desire to reaffirm gender difference. For on the face of it, the bodily changes associated with the menopause make women more 'masculine': levels of oestrogen, the stereotypical 'female' hormone, fall, and women no longer menstruate or have the potential to bear children. Such changes can be perceived as a threat to established gender divisions. Evidence to support this idea comes from the shifting justifications given for hormone replacement therapy. These shifts – as well as the proselytising zeal with which clinicians advocate HRT in the face of considerable uncertainty about its long-term costs and benefits – expose the evident concern to maintain what is seen as the biological basis of 'femininity' at all costs.

Moreover, powerful pharmaceutical interests stand to profit from hormonal treatments. According to the American journalist and author Gail Sheehy, in 1991 $750 million of oestrogen products were sold in the USA:

Drug companies anticipate that these hormones will account for close to a billion-dollar market in 1992. With the baby boom bulge projected to add over half a million women to the midlife population each year for the rest of the decade, the menopause market is becoming big business.[5]

Deficient or Just Different?

The World Health Organization has defined the menopause as 'the permanent cessation of menstruation, resulting from the loss of ovarian follicular activity'. Periods stop, and a mature egg is no longer released by the ovary once a month. The menopause can be pinpointed by backdating, after a year has elapsed without periods, the World Health Organization recommends. Because the loss of ovarian function is seen as the definitive characteristic of the menopause, women who have their ovaries removed are deemed to become surgically menopausal from the date of the operation. Women who have stopped menstruating because they have had a hysterectomy are not classed as menopausal if their ovaries remain in working order. Most women in the West experience menopause around the age of fifty, although the range, from thirty-five to fifty-nine, is wide.

What has so captured the imagination of biomedical researchers and clinicians is the hormonal changes that happen at this time. During the reproductive years, various cells within the ovary produce sex steroids: oestradiol, with smaller amounts of oestrone, are the major oestrogens. Androgens, mainly androstenedione and testosterone, are also produced. As the egg-producing, or follicular, cells grow quiescent, oestradiol decreases to perhaps 10 per cent of its previous level. Levels of other hormones also fall, but less dramatically.

A period of chemical readjustment ensues. After the menopause, oestrogens come mostly from the ability of fat cells to convert adrenal hormones, notably androstenedione, to oestrogens, mainly oestrone. So fatter postmenopausal women have higher oestrogen levels than thinner ones. Diet, exercise, drinking and smoking all have different – perhaps interacting – effects on hormone levels after the menopause.

These bald facts tell us little, however, about the significance

127

of these physiological changes, and many remarkably different interpretations have been put upon them. One school of thought, promoted particularly by feminist primatologists and anthropologists, begins with the 'grandmother hypothesis'. In this view, menopause has evolved because it maximises the reproductive output of the woman and her close kin. Through her labour and experience, the postmenopausal grandmother contributes to the survival of her children and their children. Evidence in favour of this idea comes from a recent study of the Hadza hunter-gatherers in Tanzania.[6] Post-reproductive Hadza women specialise in the collection of tubers which are a nutritious and valuable source of food, but difficult to dig up. Younger women with children do not have the time to harvest them. The older women spend more time gathering food, and bring in more than their younger relatives. So, through their skilled labour, the older women greatly enhance their kin's food supply. Menopause is not, then, a disease or a debilitating state, but a valued stage in a human life which first arose because it carried evolutionary advantages.

By contrast, other researchers have argued that menopause is an unfortunate side-effect of our extended lifespan – a view that fits well with HRT pioneer Robert Wilson's belief that menopause is an abnormal state of being. These biologists claim that our ancestors would not have lived long enough to experience it.[7] In this view, menopause is a 'deficiency disease' consequent on our pampered Western lifestyle. One of Britain's leading exponents of hormone replacement therapy, John Stevenson, a consultant endocrinologist at the Wynn Institute in London, says that women are 'hormone deficient for a third of their lives'.[8]

This view has been widely publicised. As the American sociologist Dorothy Nelkin points out, Wilson's attempts to promote hormone replacement therapy in the popular press were very successful. His diagnosis of menopause as a disease susceptible to hormonal cure was taken up with such alacrity, she argues, because his ideas converged 'with journalists' perceptions of prevailing social values; in this case, the popular fantasy of remaining forever young'.[9]

The Great Safety Debate

By the early 1970s in the USA, half of women aged fifty-five to sixty-four and a third of women aged sixty-five to seventy-four were taking oestrogen in the belief that it would keep them young and 'feminine'.[10] With such a large study population to hand, epidemiologists began to look at the links between hormone replacement therapy and the risk of various diseases. The current controversy erupted in 1975, with the publication of two American studies suggesting that women on oestrogen therapy were much more likely to develop cancer of the endometrium, the lining of the womb. By 1980 virtually all US researchers agreed that oestrogen replacement therapy increases the risk by three- to sixfold, depending on dose and duration of use.

British researchers were more sceptical of the risks. They advocated adding progestogen to the oestrogen during the last five to thirteen days of the monthly treatment to counteract the effects of oestrogen. Prominent British gynaecologists such as John Studd at King's College Hospital in London argued that this abolishes the increased risk of endometrial cancer.[11] Yet combined oestrogen and progestogen preparations are not universally prescribed today, and remain controversial, for several reasons.

There is some evidence to suggest that oestrogens (especially oestradiol) may increase the risk of breast cancer, and that adding progestogens to the mix further increases the risk. Progestogens may also increase the risk of cardiovascular disease, or obliterate the putative benefit of oestrogen. Moreover, adding progestogens for a few days each month means that postmenopausal women continue to experience a monthly bleed, something that some older women say they wish to avoid. Enthusiasts for hormone replacement therapy regularly speak of the problems of poor 'patient compliance'.[12] One way round this, advocated by Stevenson, is to implant the hormones under the skin, so that the woman cannot refrain from taking them. He is also experimenting with giving progestogen continuously, to avoid the cyclical bleeding.[13]

Clinicians have countered a wave of public concern about

the potential risks of hormone replacement therapy by promoting its benefits. Tracing the history of the controversy, Patricia Kaufert and Sonja McKinlay note the shift away from a concern with the alleviation of menopause itself.[14] Rather than being an effective, short-term treatment for distressing symptoms – the hot flushes and night sweats – hormone replacement therapy started to be advocated instead as a protection against cardiovascular disease and osteoporosis – the gradual thinning of bone that makes the elderly more liable to fractures.

What is HRT For?

Cardiovascular disease is the leading cause of death among British women, so an important question for public health policy is whether hormone replacement therapy can reduce the risk of women dying from heart attacks or strokes. Some – but not all – studies suggest that taking oestrogen reduces a postmenopausal woman's risk of coronary heart disease (CHD) by up to 60 per cent. Yet benefit does not seem to be linked to the duration of therapy, and is more marked in current users compared to past users. The apparent benefit might be the result of a selection bias, if healthier women are more likely to be users of hormone replacement therapy, argues British epidemiologist Kay-Tee Khaw of the University of Cambridge.[15]

No one yet knows how oestrogen might benefit the heart. The best guess is that it works by increasing blood levels of the 'good' form of cholesterol, high-density lipoproteins, which ferry cholesterol away from artery walls. But there are signs that this benefit is lost when progestogen is given as well, to reduce the risk of endometrial cancer. The effect of adding progestogen remains 'a major uncertainty', Khaw concludes.

Oestrogen therapy is also advocated for older women to prevent or slow the loss of bone. After the age of about thirty-five the bones of both men and women gradually become less dense and more fragile. The rate of bone loss accelerates in women after the menopause; this partly explains why elderly women are at greater risk of suffering from 'brittle bones' or osteoporosis. But the risk of developing osteoporosis also depends on how dense the bones had become at their youthful peak. Osteoporosis is virtually unknown among black women, for instance, because they develop much denser bones to start with. Genetics, exercise and diet all seem to play a part.

But advocates of hormone replacement therapy have focused on just one factor in the equation: the bone loss after menopause. Even so, Khaw points out, 'the potential value that perimenopausal oestrogen use may have for preventing osteoporotic fractures, most of which occur after the age of 75 years, is still debatable since there are no long-term primary prevention trials'. Moreover, she argues, the available data suggest that women would have to keep taking oestrogen for at least five years, and more probably ten or more, to reduce their fracture risk significantly. The trouble is, the longer the woman takes hormones, the greater her risk of developing breast cancer seems to be. Again, it is not clear whether adding progestogens influences fracture risk.

'Good News' for Women?

In the current wave of enthusiasm for hormone replacement therapy, these questions of evidence are brushed aside. 'HRT delivers spectacular benefits,' claims John Stevenson. 'Female sex hormones are incredibly good news.'[16] As Germaine Greer argues eloquently in *The Change*, the medical profession has consistently ignored the notion that the menopause is a process that can be modified by the way women live. Scant attention has been paid to the women who sail through the menopause with little bother, and live to a healthy old age: 'The obstacle to understanding here is the defect that disfigures all gynaecological investigation; we do not know enough about the well woman to understand what has gone wrong with the sick one.'[17]

Khaw argues that there is evidence to support Greer's view. Cross-cultural comparisons suggest that neither hot flushes nor chronic diseases such as osteoporosis are inevitable consequences of the menopause. Studies conducted in different countries using comparable methodology have found that while 65 per cent of Canadian women report hot flushes at some time during the menopause, only 20 per cent of Japanese women do.[18] Psychological symptoms such as depression and tiredness were reported by a quarter of Dutch menopausal women, but only 5 to 10 per cent of Japanese women. 'We do not know why such wide variations in symptoms occur, nor do we understand the specific mechanisms; in particular, the role of oestrogen deficiency is still debated,' Khaw claims.

The part oestrogen plays in the development of osteoporosis and heart disease is similarly unclear. For instance, Japanese women tend to have lower levels of oestrogen than do Caucasian women, yet the incidence of heart disease is much lower in Japan. And the widely accepted postmenopausal acceleration in the rate of coronary heart disease is 'dismissed as myth' by Hugh Tunstall-Pedoe, director of the cardio-vascular epidemiology unit at the University of Dundee. He has not found marked changes in the incidence of heart disease at around the age of fifty – quite the contrary: 'His logarithmic plot of coronary heart mortality in women in the United Kingdom shows no change in gradient around age 50,' reports the *British Medical Journal*.[19] Women in their sixties, long past the menopause, still have lower rates of death from CHD than their male contemporaries.

There is even the suggestion that oestrogen may have nothing to do with younger women's relative protection from heart disease. A Finnish study published in *Circulation*, a journal of the American Heart Association, suggests that it is high blood levels of iron that increase the risk of a heart attack.[20] Iron may interact with the 'bad' form of cholesterol, low-density lipoproteins, in a way that promotes the formation of fatty deposits on arterial walls. Oestrogen may protect younger women only indirectly, by triggering menstruation. Iron is lost with the blood, reducing levels of the metal in the bloodstream and so lessening the risk of heart disease. According to this theory, iron accumulates once periods stop, so increasing risk.

Preventing Bone Loss

As for osteoporosis, British women today are twice as likely to suffer hip fractures as were their peers of the same age thirty years ago – a change that is impossible to link to any change in oestrogen levels. A decline in habitual levels of exercise, diet or time spent out in the sun seems much more likely to be responsible. Epidemiological studies suggest that a meal of fatty fish each day, or fifteen minutes in the sun (so enhancing vitamin D levels), reduces fracture risk by a fifth. Such evidence suggests, Khaw claims, that 'while menopause may be a risk factor, there are other determinants which are likely to have a more profound influence'. Much more needs to be learnt about the interconnections between lifestyle, disease and hormones. Diet, cigarette smoking and physical activity can all have major effects. For instance, cigarette smoking may exacerbate bone loss: it seems to reduce oestrogen levels and increase androgen levels in postmenopausal women, and perhaps in younger women too.

Recently, biomedical researchers have begun to study not just bone loss in older women, but how bone is built up in youth and middle age. Several new studies suggest that exercise in girls and women who have not reached the menopause can significantly increase the mineral density of their skeletons.[21] Moreover, menopausal women who are even moderately active seem to have denser bones than their more slothful contemporaries. Regularly attending a keep-fit class can apparently rebuild bone, even in women in their fifties or sixties, according to recent research.[22]

Vegetarian diets, perhaps especially those high in soy-bean products (such as tofu, miso, boiled soy-beans), may reduce the risk of both breast cancer and heart disease.[23] This possibility stems from the discovery that certain plant foods contain chemicals known as phytoestrogens, which act as weak oestrogens. This could help to explain why Japanese women, with a diet rich in tofu, appear to be less troubled by the menopause.

Drinking alcohol, in moderate amounts, may also raise oestrogen levels in postmenopausal women, and so help to explain why moderate drinkers have a lower risk of heart attack. Judith Gavaler of the University of Pittsburgh found that women who drank three to six glasses of wine, beer or mixed alcoholic drinks a week had higher oestrogen levels than women of similar age who abstained.[24] Alcohol appears to stimulate the conversion of androgens from the adrenal glands into oestradiol, the form of oestrogen typically given to women in HRT. A 'comfortable' body figure can also raise oestrogen levels above those of thinner women, because fat tissues convert androgens produced by the adrenal glands and ovaries after menopause into oestrogens.

Finally, we understand relatively little about what taking oestrogen supplements actually does to the body. The supplements alter more than oestrogen levels: they also decrease androgen levels and increase cortisol levels, for instance – and hormonal changes might have consequences for other bodily systems.

In this sea of uncertainty, women risk being forced to board ship under the flag of HRT. There are now dozens of different preparations on the market, with no long-term knowledge of the side-effects of any of them. Khaw points out that no one knows whether data on the benefits and risks of the early, most popular preparations can be generalised to the compounds now on offer. Moreover, she argues, 'individual women and their medical practitioners need to be clear about their main reasons for the use of hormone replacement therapy: whether for short term relief of symptoms or for longer term prophylaxis'. Different formulations, delivery systems and duration of use may be more appropriate, depending on why a woman is taking hormones.

Addicted to Hormones?

What would happen if everyone were to be clear about the reasons for hormone replacement therapy? Might this threaten to expose unexamined ideological concerns driving the most proselytising spokesmen for HRT, and many women consumers of the drugs too? As Wilson trumpeted decades ago, HRT's importance for many lies in its putative ability to keep a woman young, attractive, even-tempered and compliant.

Pushing the idea that oestrogen makes women 'feel good' to its logical extreme, a London gynaecologist and a specialist in addictive behaviour recently argued that women on oestrogen replacement therapy might become 'dependent' on the drug, rather like heroin addicts.[25] Susan Bewley and Thomas Bewley speculated in *The Lancet* that if HRT promotes feelings of well-being, it 'raises concerns about its dependence potential'. They think this possibility all the more likely because HRT 'is used to treat conditions that are part of the normal ageing process and it is promoted in the non-medical press and media as a drug that maintains youth'.

HRT advocates such as John Studd complained when *The Times* reported the *Lancet* story; Studd hailed oestrogen therapy for the postmenopausal woman as 'probably the most important advance in preventive medicine in the western world for half a century'.[26] But in a letter to *The Times*, Studd went on to claim remarkable psychological benefits for the drugs. Hormone replacement therapy, he asserted, lifts depression, elevates mood, even reignites sexual interest. It is no coincidence that Studd is also enthusiastic about adding testosterone to the hormonal cocktail given to older women, arguing that it increases sexual fantasies and sexual drive in postmenopausal women (see Chapter 1). In his advocacy of testosterone for women, Studd is consistent; if hormone replacement therapy is fundamentally about keeping a woman 'womanly' and sexually receptive, testosterone is the hormone of choice. Most sexologists link that hormone, more than any other, with sexual desire in women.

Yet the standard prescription is an oestrogen–progestogen mix. It is almost as if to add testosterone would be to acknowledge the sexual agenda implicit in the idea of HRT. Moreover, it would blur, rather than reinforce, hormonally defined gender boundaries: the idea of giving the 'male' hormone to women whose 'femininity' has already supposedly been made perilously borderline by a decline in oestrogen levels is too threatening for most clinicians to contemplate.

Do Men Have a Menopause?

Also revealing is the relative lack of interest in hormone replacement therapy for men. Osteoporosis is by no means unknown in men, and Khaw's work has shown that the more free testosterone an older man has in his blood, the denser his bones tend to be. She also cites evidence – against the received wisdom – that higher testosterone levels are linked to lower cholesterol levels, and hence a lower risk of heart disease. In a recent trial, researchers at Newcastle General Hospital found a 6 per cent increase in the density of bone in the spine of men with osteoporosis treated with testosterone for three years.[27] What more evidence do clinicians need to inspire them to advocate hormonal supplements for middle-aged men?

Quite a lot, it would seem. A feature article in *The Sunday Times* in 1992 described the notion as 'a radical and largely unknown treatment for loss of male virility and other problems of middle-age'.[28] A pioneer of the treatment, Malcolm Carruthers, runs a 'Hormone Healthcare Clinic' in London's Harley Street. He claims that men suffer from a 'viropause' equivalent to the menopause, with symptoms ranging from depression, hot flushes, lack of energy and sex drive to night sweats and circulatory problems, and that this can be cured by hormone replacement therapy. Carruthers's colleagues are sceptical, claiming that 'the male menopause is a myth and [that] administering testosterone can have dangerous side effects'. They mention prostate cancer.

The British sexologist Alan Riley cites the evidence that testosterone levels in men decline from the age of fifty, while oestrogen levels rise.[29] 'This physiological change is probably the reason why breast enlargement is common in elderly men.' Yet he concludes that hormone levels remain 'within the normal range' in most cases. Clinicians seem to be reluctant to define men as 'hormonally deficient' in their advancing years, despite the acknowledgement that there is a steady decline in testosterone levels from the fifties onwards. Changes in the sexual behaviour of older men tends to be regarded as natural and unproblematic – not a sign of hormonal imbalance, as in women. For instance, John Bancroft recently urged caution in the use of testosterone supplements for men, arguing that it is normal for older men to have a less rapid and full erection, to have difficulty in regaining an erection once lost, and to have fewer erections during sleep. He said these symptoms were 'much more likely to be related to stress' than to hormones.[30]

Writing in *The Sunday Telegraph*, James LeFanu argues that we need to know whether Carruthers's treatment 'is curing a genuine deficiency' or whether 'it is just a hormonal tonic', in which case 'it is ethically highly dubious'. LeFanu quotes Chris Thompson, a British psychiatrist: 'Treating something called the male menopause with such a powerful hormone fills me with horror.'[31] There is the sense that playing around with maleness is too risky, that the hormone is too hot to handle. 'Androgens are very dangerous things,' Stevenson recently remarked at a conference. 'Testosterone is the major cause of premature heart disease and world war.'[32] Even Fay Weldon takes up the theme, in her novel *Life Force*:

> ... when oestrogen levels sink in a woman, it is safe for society to give her hormone replacement therapy, which keeps a female female, soft, sweet and smiling, but antisocial to give the ageing man testosterone injections, for if you do he runs round raping women and hitting other men on the head. What a bummer![33]

In Decline or in Her Prime?

Cultural views on the nature of ageing profoundly shape a woman's perceptions of the menopause. As Marcha Flint puts it: 'whether menopause is viewed as reward or punishment may be critical to women's experience'.[34] Women in Mayan villages actually look forward to the menopause, because it brings freedom from years of childbearing, according to Yewoubdar Beyene, an anthropologist at the University of California in San Francisco.[35] The traditional symptoms of menopause seem to be absent, too. When she asked women about hot flushes, she drew blank stares. 'People thought I was out of my mind going around asking these questions.'

Some researchers have argued that these women have a painless menopause because their continual childbearing and breastfeeding have altered their hormones; it is conceivable that high levels of the hormones prolactin and oxytocin in breastfeeding women might mask the hormonal fluctuations around menopause.[36] But Beyene has also studied peasant women on the Greek island of Evia, who had roughly the same number of children as American women, yet suffered few of the symptoms linked to menopause in the United States. Like the Mayan women, the Greek women did not suffer hot flushes, and had few negative notions about menopause – perhaps, Beyene speculates, because their culture does not idealise youth. She concludes: 'Menopause is part of being a woman, but the menopausal experience is shaped by culture.'

Medical concepts can have a powerful impact on women's ideas about themselves. The anthropologist Emily Martin points to the metaphors of economy and production that are used to describe women's bodies.[37] Menstruation is seen as failed production, childbirth as production itself, and menopause as the end of production. Her interviews suggest that educated middle-class women are more alienated from their bodies because they have taken on board these damaging medical metaphors, while working-class women are more likely to resist the experts' view, and to feel less distanced from their bodies as a result.

Another anthropologist, Margaret Lock, has explored the changing attitudes to menopause in Japan.[38] There, menopause has traditionally been seen as a gradual transition, a part of ageing, marked by bodily changes rarely linked with menopause in the West – greying hair, worsening eyesight or failing memory, for instance. Moreover, in Japan, the end of menstruation itself is regarded as only a small and relatively insignificant part of the life-cycle transition.

Recently, however, the Japanese press has begun to talk of menopausal 'syndrome', often describing it as 'a disease of modernity' and as 'a luxury disease affecting women with too much time on their hands who run to doctors with their insignificant complaints'. The Japanese government, reluctant to finance facilities for the elderly, 'calls on traditional Confucian values of filial piety' to justify its position. In the context of a society driven by the work ethic, the focus on 'laziness' and 'luxury' makes sense. Yet there is counter-pressure to establish the 'syndrome' as a disease in need of treatment. Japanese gynaecologists, working in private clinics, now actively promote HRT for menopausal women. Their income has fallen as childbirth has shifted to specialist hospitals, and contraception has reduced the abortion rate. Looking for patients, the gynaecologists have begun to advertise, targeting older women specifically, and women's groups have now begun to discuss the menopause and its treatment.

In the West, very different symbolic meanings have become linked to menopause. As Lock points out: 'current western ideology emphasises loss, especially of sexual attractiveness, leading to depression and withdrawal'. This cultural comparison shows, she argues, that 'any effort to divorce the biology of menopause from the meanings, both ideological and individual, that are attributed to the associated social transition are, in clinical circumstances at least, inherently fraught with danger'.

A Feminist Line on HRT?

In view of all this, it becomes increasingly difficult to formalise what the feminist responses to hormone replacement therapy should be. Sociologists Patricia McCrea and Gerald Markle point to fascinating differences between the stance taken by American and British feminists.[39] In the late 1960s and early 1970s, they say, feminists in the USA began to challenge the standard medical view of menopause, and to argue that menopause was not a disease, but a natural process of ageing. The Americans claimed that medical views of menopause serve as a form of social control; if women are perceived as physically and emotionally handicapped by menstruation and menopause, they cannot and may not compete with men. As a result, US feminists have, by and large, opposed the routine use of oestrogen replacement therapy. Health and consumer groups joined feminists in their opposition to the hormonal treatment.

Yet in Britain some feminists and consumer groups have vigorously endorsed hormone replacement therapy, and castigated doctors for being unenthusiastic. Consumer groups in Britain back HRT as a consumer right. The Consumers' Association's new guide, *Understanding HRT and the Menopause*, is written by a doctor who believes there is a lack of balanced information about the risks and benefits of HRT in Britain. 'It is significant', he argues, 'that only 10 per cent of menopausal women use the therapy here, as opposed to 80 per cent in the US.'[40]

Some British feminists have seen the medical establishment's slowness to take up HRT as a sign that doctors are indifferent to women's health and keen to label female patients neurotic. McCrea and Markle credit Wendy Cooper, a journalist and medical writer, with promoting hormone replacement therapy in Britain. In her book *No Change*, published in 1975, Cooper claimed that the 'natural process' view of menopause was an excuse for 'benign neglect' on the part of the medical profession.[41] And although Germaine Greer has recently produced a powerful case against HRT, *The Change* has met with considerable disparagement. In an article in *The Sunday Times* headlined 'Farewell, Witchy Woman', journalist Helen Fielding claimed that Greer 'went on so much about the virtues of life as a wrinkled crone, hag or harridan, that she took the change back several decades'.[42]

Why this disparity? Why have American feminists been generally suspicious of hormone replacement therapy, while their British sisters seem to be welcoming it? McCrea and Markle proffer several explanations. Women in both countries try to counteract the stigma of menopause, but 'in the US, feminists have tried to neutralise the stigma by claiming that menopause is normal and not a disease; in Britain, women claim that menopausal problems are "real" and not just in their heads'.

There are also structural differences in the health care systems of the two countries that influence feminists' responses to medical innovation. In the nationalised National Health Service in Britain, the GP is a gatekeeper, discouraging new or 'unnecessary' treatments. In contrast, private American medicine, where the physician operates as a small businessman on a fee-for-service basis, creates an environment ripe for what has been called 'medical imperialism'.

Most interesting, however, are the ideological differences that distinguish women's movements on both sides of the Atlantic. In the USA, McCrea and Markle argue, feminist groups are best seen as 'free-floating', 'not aligned with any particular political party or class movement'. In this situation, they suggest, 'the locus of women's oppression is seen as rooted, not in social class, but in biological inferiority arguments'. As a result, American feminists have tried to show that differential socialisation, not biological difference, accounts for women's inferior status. In Britain, on the other hand, feminists tend to be more closely aligned with the socialist movement, and have tended to see the roots of women's oppression in the structure of capitalist societies, and so to give the biological debate less priority. As McCrea and Markle suggest: 'it has been individual feminists, and not a whole social movement, who have militated for ERT [HRT] in Great Britain'.

All the same, Gail Sheehy's book on the menopause, *Silent Passage*, was a bestseller in the United States as well as in Britain, and it can hardly be said to be a critique of HRT. Sheehy claims that feminists who believe in 'cultural determinism' deny that 'our behaviour is influenced by the biochemical balance in our bodies', and are 'frozen in an outdated era of feminism': 'These polemicists seriously misrepresent the fledgling movement to bring menopause out of the closet. Beware of this logic when you encounter it . . . It can make [those feminists] more dangerous than the wrong drug.' Sheehy claims that these dangerous women ignore 'a host of new data' from animal studies (she mentions hyaenas) that demonstrate 'how fickle behaviour can be depending upon the amount of male or female hormone present in either sex'.[43]

A Woman's Right to Choose?

So what should women do? Sheehy argues that 'there is no right or wrong' about taking HRT. Every woman must 'choose her route'. But behind the valorisation of choice lie many unanswered questions, not least 'what constitutes helpful advice to women', as the historian Jane Lewis has pointed out.[44] At issue here is the very nature of the doctor–patient relationship. In the 1970s the American medical establishment railed against the Federal Drug Administration's decision to require that HRT manufacturers insert a warning on the cancer risks with each package of oestrogen. The clinicians claimed that such a warning would destroy their patients' trust. Medical authorities also condemned the media's eagerness to report research findings on the cancer risks of HRT, arguing that this unnecessarily 'alarmed' the public. Yet at the same time, medical journals were advising change in the relationship between doctor and patient. 'Physicians were told that estrogen therapy was a case in which the tradition of the compliant patient was inappropriate,' Kaufert and McKinlay report. The motive behind this change was 'the practice of defensive medicine' in the face of possible litigation from disgruntled patients.

This advice has now been widely echoed in the British medical press. In 1989, for instance, a free newspaper for doctors, *GP*, warned general practitioners to 'leave HRT choice up to the patient'.[45] John Woodward, a GP in Sidcup, shared his worries about the 'contraindications' of hormone replacement therapy: 'The list is formidable and includes currently breast and endometrial cancer, fibroids, "lumps" in the breasts or pelvis, liver disease, familial hyperlipidaemia and otosclerosis.' How, he mused, 'do we know whether or not a woman has any of these? How many doctors enquire about familial deafness and do liver function tests, a lipid profile, mammograms, endometrial biopsy and pelvic ultrasound before starting a woman on HRT?' He goes on: 'You can be quite sure, in these days of heightened patient expectation, that if a woman develops complications you will be blamed for starting her on hormones without warning her about the possible

142

consequences of the treatment.' Just ask yourself, he says, 'how long you spend discussing the contraindications with the last woman you started on HRT'.

Woodward and his fellow GPs realise the serious implications of their situation. Their solution is deceptively straightforward: The 'pros and cons' should be 'discussed sensibly' and – most importantly – 'a clear record made of the consultation'. Woodward suggests that women should be regarded as 'responsible people' and treated 'as partners in their own medical treatment'. Obviously, 'an eye will have to be kept on them'. But, he concludes: 'If doctors are honest with their patients about the risks and benefits, I think they should let women make the final decision for themselves.'

Buried within all this soul-searching are conundrums for the woman on the receiving end. It is easy to say that women should adopt a more aggressive, activist stance towards their own health care, and should demand more information. Yet women must continue to depend on medical expertise, and the medical profession continues to define, by and large, what the risks and benefits are. Sheehy does not appear to see this as problematic, as she describes how her affluent, well-informed acquaintance 'Meredith' manages her body to juggle 'benefits' and 'risks'. Meredith decides: 'Well, hell, if I know hormones are going to protect my heart, my mind and my bones, I guess I can monitor my breasts with mammography and my uterus with ultrasound and see how it goes.'

But at issue is more than access to information and state-of-the-art medical diagnostics. For as we have seen, medical knowledge is itself partly shaped by implicit judgements about how women should be, and about what hormonal profile is compatible with real femininity. In this situation, it becomes almost impossible for women to resist such medical definitions. As Patricia Kaufert has argued, a key issue becomes the extent to which women have control over the diagnostic process.[46] It might help, as Lewis argues, if women had access to 'a more sophisticated and up-to-date digest of the medical research, which is complicated, often contradictory and rapidly changing'.[47] But as the notion that individuals are responsible for their own health gains ground in a market-led health system, women are increasingly pressured to be seen to be doing something for their health, and actively managing their bodies, even in the face of possible misgivings about the options available to them.

Tamoxifen on Trial

The row over a new hormonal drug, tamoxifen, highlights the dilemmas women face. Tamoxifen, an anti-oestrogen, has been used since 1971 to treat breast cancers – many breast tumours grow faster in the presence of oestrogen. In 1991, cancer researchers proposed to launch a large-scale clinical trial to see whether tamoxifen could prevent, as well as treat, breast cancer. This would entail giving a powerful hormonal drug to thousands of healthy women. Trevor Powles at the Royal Marsden Hospital was an enthusiastic campaigner for tamoxifen. Writing in *New Scientist* he suggested that post-menopausal women could be given a cocktail of oestrogen, progestogen and tamoxifen

> to reduce or prevent cancers of the breast, ovary and uterus; heart disease; and osteoporosis. Is this approach a danger-ous interference with nature, or the correction of a design fault? The answers lie only in carrying out clinical trials with healthy women.[48]

Powles and his colleagues offered healthy women over 35 with a family history of breast cancer the following deal: for ten years, the doctors would screen the women for breast can-cer, ovarian cancer, osteoporosis and high blood cholesterol. In return, for five years the women would have to take a pill daily, which, unbeknown to them, contained either tamoxifen or a placebo. 'To our surprise,' writes Powles, 'more than half of the eligible women agreed to join the experiment.'

The trouble started, however, when animal experiments suggested that tamoxifen causes liver cancer in rats and might do so in humans too. The Medical Research Council decided it could not immediately endorse the plan to give a potentially dangerous drug to healthy women. Yet many medical journalists in Britain attacked the MRC for its caution, arguing that women were being denied the right to choose to participate in the trial.[49] 'Choice' in almost any context is increasingly regarded as the ultimate good.

The doctors' new-found emphasis on 'letting the woman decide' merely throws the responsibility back on to the marketplace: let the buyer beware. Meanwhile, new treatments for the menopausal woman are in the pipeline, including ovarian transplants to restore fertility and delay the menopause indefinitely. The mere availability of such techniques will put great pressure on women to accept them.

Already, according to Sheehy, MP Teresa Gorman, HRT-evangelist and founder of the Amarant Trust – named after the Greek *amarantos*, 'unfading' – travels round the country 'telling women that if they want to keep the older man from leaving home for a dolly bird they, too, will get smart and use HRT'.

CONCLUSIONS

W hy, asks the American journalist Barbara Ehrenreich wryly, is the study of innate differences 'such a sexy, well-funded topic right now, which happens to be a time of organised feminist challenge to the ancient sexual divisions of power?'[1] There is a hidden agenda in research on hormonal and neurological differences between women and men: hormones and their target nerve cells are standing in for something else. Projected on to hormones and the brain are many of the current anxieties surrounding debates about difference and equality.

The fear inspired by the perception of the uncertainty and instability of social identity becomes readily transposed on to those traditional symbols of 'otherness', women and sexual 'deviants'. The search for a grounding of identity in the hormonal milieu of the fetal brain is one attempt to resolve these persistent anxieties about who we are, and how we should be.

Larger cultural concerns account for the fact that hormonal explanations are applied so selectively – most often in connection with the behaviour of women, sexual minorities, violent

147

criminal offenders and the mentally ill; and (rarely) to inefficient shift workers. This pattern of hormonal explanations is
revealing. If these individuals are, at the extreme, regarded as
victims of deranged hormones, people not so categorised are
reaffirmed as stable, rational, self-directing.

Women – as Carol Smart, professor of sociology at the
University of Leeds, has argued – remain constituted in bodily
terms. She points to contemporary versions of nineteenth-
century issues: 'the introduction of evidence on premenstrual
tension into criminal trials, the more general assertions of
mind/body instability, and the incarceration of women who
have broken the "gender contract" by failing to marry or have
children'. All these examples, she suggests,

> transport us into a field of understanding in which women
> are always already problematic. It matters not whether one
> is arguing that PMT should or should not be allowed in;
> what matters is the way in which women are already
> framed by the very legitimacy of asking such a question.[2]

Contemporary women are most often symbolically loaded
with the cultural angst of the times. Their role as the 'other' in
patriarchal systems makes the pressures on them particularly
intense. Feminist theorists have shown how concepts of civil
society are built around the political constructions of what it
means to be a man or a woman. The work of Carole Pateman,
professor of political science at the University of California at
Los Angeles, has shown how the classic contract theorists

> presented sexual difference as the political difference
> between freedom (men) and subordination (women).
> Women were held by nature to lack the characteristics
> required for participation in political life, and citizenship
> has been constructed in the male image. Women, our bodies
> and distinctive capacities, represented all that citizenship
> and equality are not. 'Citizenship' has gained its meaning
> through the exclusion of women, that is to say (sexual)
> 'difference'.[3]

In fact, Pateman argues, women became incorporated into the

political order, but as subordinates, as the 'different' sex, as 'women', in a society where men were the 'individuals', the 'citizens' of political theory. Thus, she maintains, the vital question now is 'how to subvert and change the manner in which women have already been incorporated'.

Today, ideas about women may even have a symbolic role in the workplace, as fears of disempowerment in an increasingly machine-driven, alienating world increase. Images of man as machine, as a tiny cog in the vast industrialised and bureaucratised hierarchies of work, arose early in the Victorian era and retain their potency today. With technological advance, the very borderline between man and machine is now perceived to be under threat, inspiring Hollywood films such as *Robocop*, constructed round the recurrent science-fiction fantasy of the cyborg.[4] Echoing this theme, Alan Wolfe, of the New School for Social Research in New York, articulates fears that artificial intelligence heralds the computer's superiority to the human mind.[5] In this climate, it may be strangely comforting to sustain the construction of women as hormonally driven: men, by comparison, can then appear balanced and in control.

Managing the Body

The intensification of work in recent decades also increases pressure on the citizen, male and female alike, as worker, and on the need for self-discipline and self-control. As Michel Foucault and others have pointed out, our recent past is notable for the internalisation of social control; policing the body, ensuring its efficiency, has become internalised, and is now seen as the responsibility of the individual.[6] Achieving such control becomes all the more difficult as it is counterposed to exhortations from advertisers to indulge in consumption tied to new forms of lifestyle and leisure, to give way to impulse and hedonistic desire, in the present-day free-market economy. The image of the consumer also conceals the power relations at work behind the scenes. The individual seen as consumer exists as a disconnected, self-contained unit, stripped of any notion of relationship – as Marilyn Strathern, professor of social anthropology at the University of Cambridge, puts it: 'an enterprise with nothing to do but manage his or her affairs'.[7]

'Enterprise' became a key word in the late 1980s and early 1990s, connoting the fusion of personal self-reliance with 'lean and fit' business organisation. Central to the ideology promulgated by successive Conservative governments, 'enterprise' formed part of the political campaign to restructure both the British economy and society. Russell Keat, a philosopher at the University of Lancaster, points out that the term not only suggests individual initiative and drive but also has an economic, corporate meaning – it implies that everything should be run as if it were a business.[8] Among the buzz words of the modern 'enterprise culture' are 'packaging' and 'consumer choice'.

Contemporary popular culture places a great emphasis on 'body management', especially by women. This is only too evident in the concern with the technologies of diet and exercise. The control of appetite and the triumph over fat, the 'working out' to tone the body and strip away surplus fat, has become a central means of the reproduction of gender relations. Such body management can also be seen to reflect women's attempts to gain control over bodies that they themselves have come to see as threatening – the source of illicit desires.

In all this the focus on the inner, and the struggle to maintain control over it, obscures the individual's lack of control over public events, and makes the prospect of engaging in organised political action to achieve greater control increasingly unimaginable. Women's cycles are seen as a biological given, something to be managed in private; if their body time prevents their slotting into public time, they are encouraged to seek hormonal treatments to correct this imbalance. Inner chemistry, not the ordering of public life, has to be adjusted.

In a similar way, today's health promotion campaigns can help to undermine women's autonomy, as deterministic ideas about hormones (as some inner force that must be managed and tamed) are combined with an equally individualised model of health as residing in 'lifestyle behaviour'. Suggestions that the body's hormonal state is 'in your hands', to be properly maintained through a sensible lifestyle, intensify the pressure to conform to some abstraction of health.

Freedom of choice?

Increasingly, the individual is represented as constituted by the choices he or she makes. Shad Helmstetter, bestselling author of the self-help book *What to Say When You Talk to Yourself*, has recently published his follow-up, *Life Choices: Manage Your Choices, Manage Your Life*, with the cover flash 'Discover Your 100 Most Important Life Choices'.[9] In a culture devoted to consumption, as Strathern has pointed out, responsibility becomes a matter of discriminating between products. This ideology of choice carries with it the image of a shopper in the supermarket of life, filling her basket according to her personal preferences. But choosing to buy Pepsi rather than Coke does not allow us to choose, or sometimes even to imagine how things might be different – to deviate from what is on offer. Moreover, people have very unequal access to power and money: some have much less opportunity to choose than others. Finally, individuals cannot in reality choose alone, somehow disconnected from their social world. 'Persons are made up of other persons', writes Strathern; as a result, choice carries with it consequences that are not always apparent from the outset.[10] Women can use HRT or take contraceptive pills for many reasons, but those choices have sequelae. As Strathern has pointed out, making choices unavoidably involves making discriminations between alternative outcomes, or ways of being.

The availability of hormone replacement therapy intensifies pressures on women to manage their bodies and take responsibility for their physical state. Increasingly, women are being sold HRT as a panacea for future health, with the implication that if they fail to continue with the medication they will have only themselves to blame if they develop heart disease or brittle bones. And because nobody in reality chooses alone, what appears to be a matter of individual choice, intimately related to her own body, may in fact primarily reflect her feelings of responsibility towards others – husbands, lovers, children, elderly parents and colleagues. These conundrums are covertly acknowledged by self-help books such as the recent BBC publication *Time of Her Life*, which repeatedly tells the reader: 'You shouldn't allow yourself to be stampeded into starting [HRT] against your will', and that she should 'avoid being pressured into anybody else's choice'.[11]

Ironically, the promotion of a heightened awareness of individual responsibility for improving health has actually increased the feeling of the precariousness of health, argues Kathryn Backett of the University of Edinburgh.[12] Uncertainty about health has grown hand in hand with health promotion; no one can be sure that a particular action will bring about the desired end in the long term, and individuals look for short-term proof (such as few illnesses or lots of energy) to reduce worry and uncertainty. Backett interviewed twenty-eight middle-class couples on several occasions to explore in depth their feelings about health and the way they lived. She found that for many individuals a fatalistic streak about health matters coexists with the notion that 'good health' is an achieved state. They are aware of being influenced by economic and political factors that constrain potential to achieve, and worry that they are not doing enough. For these people, healthiness has become a 'moral imperative', and they feel that they have to justify deviations from what is perceived as healthy behaviour in terms of other moral duties and obligations (such as paid work or childcare). Seeking medical attention, often in the form of hormonal treatments, is perceived to be one of the most powerful ways in which individuals can demonstrate that they are taking responsibility for the regulation of the body and the maintenance of health.

The present trend carries many dangers – not least that of further reinforcing the status quo with the authority of contemporary science and medicine. Just as worrying is the presentation of an ever more simplistic vision of the origin and nature of human relationships. This vision may become more difficult to challenge as biomedical theories become ever more arcane, as they shift from a focus on hormones to concentrate on brain chemistry and molecular genetics. Such scientific change does not necessarily imply advance.[13] Biomedical science in the twentieth century seems, at least to some extent, to have revived the themes and preoccupations of an earlier era.

Political science, scientific politics

An appeal to biology is a powerful rhetorical device which becomes all the more powerful when it is apparently backed by the latest research in brain sciences or human genetics. 'The real argument', writes Anne Fausto-Sterling, 'is not about biology at all – it is about the social transformations urged on our culture by activist feminists and gay rights advocates and about the oppositions such urgings have met.'[14]

The traditional image of science as something removed from the hurly-burly of everyday life, able to discover pure, objective Truth, obscures the political issues under a veil of 'facts of nature'. Sandra Harding and others argue that science is, at its core, a social activity; there is no way in which scientists can be insulated from their position as members of the human race to make direct contact with 'nature' in the raw. Inanimate nature comes to us 'culturally preconditioned as a possible object of knowledge', Harding argues:

> We cannot 'strip nature bare' to 'reveal her secrets', as conventional views have held, for no matter how long the striptease continues or how rigorous its choreography, we will always find under each 'veil' only nature-as-conceptualised-within-cultural projects; we will always (but not only) find more veils.[15]

Science can indeed produce reliable knowledge, says Harding, 'but it does so as, for better or worse, it participates in politics'. By this she means not that science is flawed or less valid than it should be; rather, that social concerns are inexorably enmeshed in scientific projects. Science is seen as a social activity not radically at odds with other kinds of human expertise.[16] How science is made to seem outside politics is what we need to understand.[17]

Politics seems to be far removed from brain anatomy. Simon LeVay speaks of 'interaction' between 'genetic differences between individuals' and 'environmental factors', but he emphasises the genetic, and predicts that scientists will soon discover genes that influence our sexual behaviour.[18] This will make it 'inevitable', he argues, that 'the perception of our own nature, in the field of sex as in all attributes of our physical and mental lives, will be increasingly dominated by concepts derived from the biological sciences'. It makes sense to think about the mind in biological terms, 'since even environmental and cultural influences on the mind operate through biological mechanisms'. The outer world comes to us via neurological and hormonal channels, so it must be reducible to such 'mechanisms'. LeVay is by no means alone in this belief: another neurobiologist, Dick Swaab, scoffed at a headline in *Science*, 'Is Homosexuality Biological?' commenting: 'It's a nonsense question – all behaviour is biological.'[19]

Life in Context

Yet these neuroscientists have an impoverished vision of the way we are. Feminists, among others, have consistently taken another point of view, one in which the rich social context of people's lives throughout their life course does not disappear from the picture. In any gender-dichotomised society, argues Ruth Hubbard, those who are born biologically female or male will live different lives, with profound consequences for the way we are in every sense. This makes it impossible to know whether biological differences between men and women exist, because 'biology and society (or environment) are interdependent and cannot be sorted out'.[20] Scientists can only catalogue similarities and differences between women and men; they cannot establish their causes.

Sandra Lipsitz Bem writes provocatively of a 'utopian' vision of a world in which 'gender polarisation' has been eradicated, where 'the distinction between male and female no longer organises either the culture or the psyche'.[21] In this world the sexes would no longer be culturally identified with different clothes, social roles, personalities, sexual and affectional partners – the very concepts of masculinity/femininity and homosexual/bisexual/heterosexual would disappear: 'We would view the biological fact of being male or female much as we now view the biological fact of being human, not as something we have to "work at"' – in the sense that we feel we have to work at being a real man or a real woman, but not a real human being. In this remarkable world, everyone would be free to develop their human potential, and gender polarisation would no longer form the foundation of anthropocentrism and the justification for the oppression of women.

Bem's imaginary world helps to convey something of the power that sex differences now hold, and the complexity of their origins. Even to speak of the interaction of the genes with the environment as an explanation for difference can be misleading. As the American developmental psychologist Susan Oyama argues, we are not the mere effects of genetic and environmental causes, but 'active beings that to some extent define our own possibilities'.[22] Humans, as well as many other animals, shape the world they live in, so they are continually altering the relationships between themselves and their context, in complex and unpredictable ways.

Oyama goes on to argue that the very judgement as to what is regarded as constructed or acquired, and what is given – as part of an individual's nature or inheritance – is open to reinterpretation. In her alternative description, what is inherited are 'developmental means' – all the interactants that enable an organism to develop, including its environment – while what is constructed are the results of this developmental process, the 'nature' of the organism. Oyama turns essentialism on its head by emphasising the ecological embeddedness of development and inheritance: 'All developed form and function, all "nature" (whether we consider it normal, healthy, adaptive, or not), is a function of that embeddedness. Nature and nurture are not alternative causes but product and process.'

All this is relevant to 'hormones' because they are still typically regarded as part of some primeval package, inherited from our brutish ancestors, which lurks under the veneer of civilisation, threatening to destroy it. Our inner bodily secrets, made visible by the penetrating gaze of science, are meant to hint at this animal inheritance. In fact, the body is not some biological entity in which scientists can discover the origins of difference. Social relations, inequalities and oppressions have become embodied in the way we are – our bodies reflect socially engendered difference. The body is constructed through developmental processes that include the social, creating differences which science misreads as foundational.

In the end, our world is inexorably relational, and so is the practice of science – quite as much as gender and sexuality, the phenomena it seeks to know. Gender and sexual orientation are not things, or 'interior states' that can be investigated by traditional scientific methods; masculine and feminine, gay and straight, are always defined against each other and continually enacted in each individual's experience of the social world. The ideology of modern scientific practice not only obscures its own social context but also presents us with a description of ourselves that is a travesty of the complex, contradictory web of interactions that make up our lives. To contest this simplification and distortion is not to be anti-science; it is to move towards a better science – towards finding ways to understand and interpret the worlds we actually create, and inhabit.

NOTES

Introduction

1. '"Raging" father killed children in home fire', *The Guardian*, 17 March 1992.
2. H. Allen, *Justice Unbalanced*, Milton Keynes: Open University Press, 1987.
3. O. Riddle, R.W. Bates and E.L. Lahr, 'Prolactin Induces Broodiness in Fowl', *American Journal of Physiology* 111 (1935): 352–60; O. Riddle, 'Prolactin or Progesterone as Key to Parental Behaviour: A Review', *Animal Behaviour* 11 (1963): 419–32.
4. P. Klopfer and J. Hailman, *An Introduction to Animal Behavior*, Englewood Cliffs, NJ: Prentice Hall, 1967.
5. E.-E. Baulieu and P. Kelly, *Hormones: From Molecules to Disease*, London: Chapman & Hall, 1990.
6. F. Berkovitch and T. Ziegler (eds), *Socioendocrinology of Primate Reproduction*, New York: Wiley-Liss, 1990.
7. E.B. Keverne, 'Primate Social Relationships: Their Determinants and Consequences', in *Advances in the Study of Behavior*, P. Slater *et al.* (eds), London: Academic Press (1992): 1–38.
8. G. Mason, 'Female Doves "Talk" to Their Ovaries', *New Scientist*, 9 January 1993: 17.
9. J.B. Hutchinson, 'How Does the Environment Influence the Behavioural Action of Hormones?', in P. Bateson (ed.), *The Development and Integration of Behaviour*, Cambridge: Cambridge University Press, 1991: 149–170.

10. Baulieu and Kelly, *Hormones;* see also E. Baulieu, Preface, in M. Haug, P.F. Brain and C. Aron (eds), *Heterotypical Behaviour in Man and Animals,* London: Chapman & Hall; 1991.

11. D. Crews, 'Diversity of Hormone–Behavior Relations in Reproductive Behavior', in J. Becker, M. Breedlove and D. Crews, *Behavioral Endocrinology,* Cambridge, MA: MIT Press, 1992, pp. 143–86.

12. D. Haraway, 'Contested Bodies', in M. McNeil (ed.), *Gender and Expertise,* London: Free Association Books, 1987: 62–76.

13. R. Sharpe and N. Skakkebaek, 'Are Oestrogens Involved in Falling Sperm Counts and Disorders of the Male Reproductive Tract?' *The Lancet,* 341: 1392–1395.

14. J. Hope, 'Why Men Are Now Half As Fertile As their Grandfathers,' 7 June 1993, *Daily Mail,* p. 18.

15. T. Laqueur, *Making Sex,* Cambridge, MA: Harvard University Press, 1990.

16. C. Eagle Russet, *Sexual Science: The Victorian Construction of Womanhood,* Cambridge, MA: Harvard University Press, 1989.

17. L. Schiebinger, *The Mind Has No Sex? Women in the Origins of Modern Science,* Cambridge, MA: Harvard University Press, 1989.

18. L. Jordanova, *Sexual Visions: Images of Gender in Science and Medicine between the Eighteenth and Twentieth Centuries,* Madison, WI: University of Wisconsin Press, 1989.

19. M. Douglas, *Natural Symbols,* London: The Cresset Press, 1970.

1: Hormones of Desire

1. J. Becker, M. Breedlove and D. Crews (eds), *Behavioral Endocrinology,* Cambridge, MA: MIT Press, 1992.

2. P. de Kruif, *The Male Hormone,* New York: Harcourt Brace, 1945.

3. M. Borell, 'Organotherapy and the Emergence of Reproductive Endocrinology', *Journal of the History of Biology* 18 (1985): 1–30.

4. D. Hamilton, *The Monkey Gland Affair,* London: Chatto & Windus, 1986.

5. D. Long Hall, 'The Critic and the Advocate: Contrasting British Views on the State of Endocrinology in the Early 1920s', *Journal of the History of Biology* 9 (1976): 269–85.

6. ibid.

7. T. Glick, 'On the Diffusion of a New Specialty: Marañón and the "Crisis" of Endocrinology in Spain', *Journal of the History of Biology* 9 (1976): 287–300.

8. D. Long Hall, 'Physiological Identity of American Sex Researchers Between the Two World Wars', in G. Geison (ed.), *Physiology in the American Context, 1850–1940,* Bethesda, MD: American Physiological Society, 1987, pp. 263–78.

9. Nelly Oudshoorn, 'On the Making of Sex Hormones: Research Materials and the Production of Knowledge', *Social Studies of Science* 20 (1990): 5–33;

NOTES

and N. Oudshoorn, 'Endocrinologists and the Conceptualisation of Sex, 1920–1940', *Journal of the History of Biology* 23 (1990): 163–86.

10. A. Riley, E. Riley and P. Brown, 'Biological Aspects of Sexual Desire in Women', *Sexual and Marital Therapy* 1 (1986): 35–42; and A. Riley, 'Sexuality and the Menopause', *Sexual and Marital Therapy* 6 (1991): 135–46.

11. R.E. Goodman, 'The Role of Androgens in Female Sexual Function and Dysfunction', *British Journal of Sexual Medicine*, August 1989: 312–15.

12. G. Vines, 'Sex, Drugs and Science', *Vogue*, March 1993: 234–6.

13. C. S. Carter, 'Hormonal Influences on Human Sexual Behavior', in Becker *et al.*, (eds), *Behavioral Endocrinology:* 131–42.

14. J.M. Dabbs and S. Mohammed, 'Male and Female Salivary Testosterone Concentrations Before and After Sexual Activity', *Physiology and Behavior* 52 (1992): 195–7.

15. Carter, 'Hormonal Influences'; J. Bancroft, *Human Sexuality and Its Problems*, 2nd edn, London: Churchill Livingstone, 1989.

16. J. Bancroft, 'Sexual Desire and the Brain', *Sexual and Marital Therapy* 3 (1988): 11–27.

17. G. Alexander and B. Sherwin, 'The Association between Testosterone, Sexual Arousal and Selective Attention for Erotic Stimuli in Men', *Hormones and Behavior* 25 (1991): 367–81.

18. A. Burris *et al.*, 'Testosterone Therapy Is Associated with Reduced Tactile Sensitivity in Human Males', *Hormones and Behavior* 25 (1991): 195–205.

19. J. Bancroft, *Human Sexuality and Its Problems*.

20. P. Schreiner-Engel *et al.*,'Low Sexual Desire in Women: The Role of Reproductive Hormones', *Hormones and Behavior* 23 (1989): 221–34.

21. J. Bancroft, 'Hormones, Sexuality and Fertility in Women', *Journal of Zoology* 213 (1987): 445–54.

22. S. Matteo and E. Rissman, 'Increased Sexual Activity during the Midcycle Portion of the Human Menstrual Cycle', *Hormones and Behavior* 18 (1984): 249–55.

23. J. Bancroft, *Human Sexuality and Its Problems*.

24. F. Purifoy and L. Koopmans, 'Androstenedione, Testosterone and Free Testosterone Concentration in Women of Various Occupations', *Social Biology* 26 (1980): 179–88.

25. G. Alexander, B. Sherwin, J. Bancroft and D. Davidson, 'Testosterone and Sexual Behavior in Oral Contraceptive Users and Nonusers: A Prospective Study', *Hormones and Behavior* 24 (1990): 388–402.

26. J. Guillebaud, *The Pill*, 4th edn, Oxford: Oxford University Press, 1991; *See also* A. Szarewski, *Hormonal Contraception: A Woman's Guide*, London: Macdonald Optima, 1991.

27. Alexander *et al.*, 'Testosterone and Sexual Behavior'.

28. A. Riley, 'Practical Issues in Androgen Therapy', *British Journal of Sexual Medicine*, September 1989): 352–6.

29. M. Walling, B.L. Andersen and S.R. Johnson, 'Hormonal Replacement Therapy for Postmenopausal Women: A Review of Sexual Outcomes and

Related Gynecological Effects', *Archives of Sexual Behaviour* 19 (1990): 119–37.

30. J. Studd *et al.*, 'Oestradiol and Testosterone Implants in the Treatment of Psychosexual Problems in the Postmenopausal Woman', *British Journal of Obstetrics and Gynaecology* 88 (1977): 314–15.
31. G. Greer, *The Change*, Harmondsworth: Penguin, 1992.
32. G. Sheehy, *The Silent Passage*, London: HarperCollins, 1993.
33. C. Dyer, 'A Panacea for Sex Offenders?', *The Guardian*, 27 May 1992.
34. S. Lonsdale, 'Sex Attacks Linked to Steroid Abuse, Say Police', *The Observer*, 19 January 1992, p. 2.
35. M. J. Cole, 'Sex Therapy – A Critical Appraisal', *British Journal of Psychiatry* 147 (1985): 337–51; and M. Cole, and W. Dryden (eds), *Sex Therapy in Britain*, Milton Keynes: Open University Press, 1988. Cole writes that until quite recently up to 90 per cent of cases of impotence (erectile failure) were thought to be the result of psychological problems. Now, he says, there is 'abundant evidence that organic conditions may be implicated' in as many as half of these cases – with the prospect of pharmaceutical treatments to supplant laborious and uncertain psychological interventions. But potential drugs now in the pipeline are intended to treat premature ejaculation and impotence by acting directly on the penis's erectile machinery. Researchers in industry acknowledge that drugs which alter desire – perhaps by exerting some chemical change in the brain – are a much more distant prospect.
36. Carter, 'Hormonal Influences', and C.S. Carter and L.L. Getz, 'Monogamy and the Prairie Vole', *Scientific American*, 268 (June 1993): 70–77.
37. H. Bloch and S. Donnelly, 'How Do Fools Fall in Love?', *Time*, 15 February 1993: 56–7.
38. D. Eyer, *Mother–Infant Bonding: A Scientific Fiction*, New Haven, CT: Yale University Press, 1993.
39. K.M. Kendrick, F. Lévy and E.B. Keverne, 'Changes in the Sensory Processing of Olfactory Signals Induced by Birth in Sheep', *Science*, 256 (1992): 833–6.
40. M. Klaus and J. Kennell, *Maternal–Infant Bonding*, St Louis MO: Mosby, 1976.

2: *Hormonal Times*

1. K. Dalton, *The Premenstrual Syndrome and Progesterone Therapy*, London: Heinemann, 1977.
2. S. Laws, *Issues of Blood: The Politics of Menstruation*, London: Macmillan, 1990.
3. S. Prendergast, *This is the Time to Grow Up*, Cambridge: Health Promotion Research Trust, 1992.
4. N. Oudshoorn, *The Making of the Hormonal Body: A Contextual History of Sex Hormones*, The Hague: CIP-Gegevens Koninklijke Bibliotheek, 1991.

NOTES

5. K. Dalton, *Once a Month*, 5th edn, London: Fontana, 1991; K. Dalton, *The Premenstrual Syndrome*, London: Heinemann, 1964.
6. H. Kennedy, *Eve Was Framed*, London: Chatto & Windus, 1992.
7. H. Fielding, 'That Time of the Month', *The Sunday Times*, 26 April 1993.
8. B. Donovan, *Hormones and Human Behaviour*, Cambridge: Cambridge University Press, 1985.
9. D. Asso, 'Physiology and Psychology of the Normal Menstrual Cycle', in M.G. Brush and E.M. Goudsmit (eds), *Functional Disorders of the Menstrual Cycle*, London: Wiley, 1988, pp. 15–36.
10. G. Sampson, 'Definitions of Premenstrual Syndrome and Related Conditions', in ibid., pp. 37–54.
11. W.R. Butt, 'New Concepts in the Endocrinology of Premenstrual Syndrome', in ibid., pp. 117–34.
12. C. Morse and L. Dennerstein, 'Cognitive Therapy for Premenstrual Syndrome', in ibid., pp. 177–90.
13. E. Goudsmit, 'Psychological Aspects of Premenstrual Symptoms', in ibid. pp. 159–76.
14. L. Birke and K. Gardner, *Why Suffer? Periods and Their Problems*, London: Virago, 1979; P. Weideger, *Female Cycles*, London: The Women's Press, 1978; B. Seaman and G. Seaman, *Women and the Crisis in Sex Hormones*, New York: Rawson Associates, 1977.

    In a small survey by Precilla Choi, a psychologist at University College London, women who exercised three times a week or more 'did not experience any deterioration in their mood or energy levels when they were in their premenstrual phase'. Those who took less exercise, or none, apparently felt worse and experienced greater fatigue. But studies such as this cannot tell us whether the women who were keen on exercise were different from the others in some way that had nothing to do with the physical exertion. *Women and Science Newsletter*, issue 5, January/February 1993, London: Science Policy Support Group.
15. A. Fausto-Sterling, *Myths of Gender*, revised edn, New York: Basic Books, 1992.
16. S. Laws, *Issues of Blood*.
17. I. Cohen, B. Sherwin and A. Fleming, 'Food Cravings, Mood and the Menstrual Cycle', *Hormones and Behavior* 21 (1987): 457–507.
18. L. Dayton, 'The Right Time for a Woman to Diet?', *New Scientist*, 25 April 1992: 15.
19. R. Weiss, 'Women's Skills Linked to Estrogen Levels', *Science News*, 26 November 1988: 341.
20. A. Fausto-Sterling, *Myths of Gender*. See also H. Gordon and P. Lee, 'No Difference in Cognitive Performance between Phases of the Menstrual Cycle,' *Psychoneuroendocrinology* 18 (1993): 521–31.
21. E. Hampson and D. Kimura, 'Sex Differences and Hormonal Influences on Cognitive Function in Humans', in J. Becker, S.M. Breedlove and D. Crews (eds), *Behavioral Endocrinology*, Cambridge, MA: MIT Press, 1992, pp 357–400.

22. C. Kitzinger, 'Barbara Sommer: Lifting the Curse', *The Psychologist*, July 1989: 297.

23. S. Shuttleworth, 'Female Circulation: Medical Discourse and Popular Advertising in the Mid-Victorian Era,' in M. Jacobus, E. Fox Keller and S. Shuttleworth (eds), *Body/Politics*, London: Routledge, 1990.

24. Ibid.

25. 'Women and the DSM', *Women and Science Newsletter*, issue 6, March/April 1993, London: Science Policy Support Group.

26. M. Rodin, 'The Social Construction of Premenstrual Syndrome', *Social Science and Medicine* 35 (1992): 49–56.

27. J. Zita, 'The Premenstrual Syndrome "Dis-easing" the Female Cycle', in N. Tuana (ed.), *Feminism and Science*, Bloomington, IN: Indiana University Press, 1989, pp. 188–210.

28. A. Gottlieb, 'American Premenstrual Syndrome: A Mute Voice', *Anthropology Today* 4 (1988): 10–13.

29. E. Martin, 'Premenstrual Syndrome: Discipline, Work, and Anger in Late Industrial Societies', in T. Buckley and A. Gottlieb (eds), *Blood Magic: The Anthropology of Menstruation*, Berkeley, CA: University of California Press, 1988.

    Many of Martin's arguments may also apply to the phenomenon of postnatal depression, also sometimes perceived as the result of the decline of progesterone at birth. Many researchers have attempted to find a link between a mother's mental state and her hormones, but without much success (e.g. R. Smith *et al.*,'Mood Changes, Obstetric Experience and Alterations in Plasma Cortisol, Beta-Endorphin and Corticotrophin Releasing Hormone during Pregnancy and Puerperium', *Journal of Psychosomatic Medicine* 34 [1990]: 53–69).

30. C. Read, 'Time of the Month? A Thing of the Past', *The Guardian*, 5 April 1993, p. 11, second section; L. Rogers, 'PMT May Be All in the Mind', *The Sunday Times*, 4 April 1993.

31. L. Sussman, 'This Woman is Premenstrual (So How Come She Feels So Good?)', *New Woman*, June 1993: 12–14; Anonymous, 'Surprise! The Good News About PMS', *Company*, June 1993: 13.

32. A. Reynolds, 'Why Women Are Angry Every Month', *The Observer*, 18 April 1993, p. 53.

33. E. Haus, and Y. Touitou, 'Principles of Clinical Chronobiology', in Y. Touitou and E. Haus (eds), *Biologic Rhythms in Clinical and Laboratory Medicine*, Berlin: Springer-Verlag, 1992, pp. 6–34.

34. J. Horne, *Why We Sleep*, Oxford: Oxford University Press, 1988.

35. A. Miles, D. Philbrick and C. Thompson (eds), *Melatonin: Clinical Perspectives*, Oxford: Oxford University Press, 1988.

36. R. Reiter, 'The Ageing Pineal Gland and Its Physiological Consequences', *BioEssays* 14 (1992): 169–75.

37. J. Arendt, 'Melatonin and the Human Circadian System,' in Miles *et al.* (eds), *Melatonin*, pp. 43–61.

38. D.F. Kripke, M.D. Drennan and J.A. Elliott, 'The Complex Circadian

Pacemaker in Affective Disorders', in Touitou and Haus (eds), *Biologic Rhythms*, pp. 265–76.

39. J. Arendt, 'The Pineal', in ibid., pp. 348–62.
40. Kripke *et al.*, 'The Complex Circadian Pacemaker'.
41. L.N. Edmunds, Jr, 'Cellular and Molecular Aspects of Circadian Oscillators: Models and Mechanisms for Biological Timekeeping', in Touitou and Haus (eds), *Biologic Rhythms*, pp. 35–54.
42. C.M. Winget, M.R.I. Soliman, D.C. Holley and J.S. Meylor, 'Chronobiology of Physical Performance and Sports Medicine', in ibid., pp. 230–42.
43. D.F. Swaab and M.A. Hofman, 'Sexual Differentiation of the Human Brain: A Historical Perspective', *Progress in Brain Research* 61 (1984): 361–74.

3: *Hormonal Havoc*

1. S. Bordo, 'Reading the Slender Body,' in M. Jacobus, E. Fox Keller and S. Shuttleworth (eds), *Body/Politics*, London: Routledge, 1990, pp. 83–112; Bordo, *Unbearable Weight*, Berkeley and Los Angeles: University of California Press, 1993.

2. R. Lloyd Parry, 'Lean years for real women', *The Sunday Times*, 10 January 1993; D.M. Gardner, P.E. Garfinkel, Schwarts and M. Thompson, 'Cultural Expectations of Thinness in Women', *Psychological Reports* 47 (1980): 483–91.

3. S. Mennell, A. Murcott and A. van Otterloo, *The Sociology of Food*, London: Sage, 1992; see also a survey of readers' attitudes to food in *Cosmopolitan*, March 1993.

4. R. Gordon, *Anorexia and Bulimia: Anatomy of a Social Epidemic*, Oxford: Basil Blackwell, 1990.

5. S. Orbach, *Fat is a Feminist Issue*, Harmondsworth: Penguin, 1978. Subtitled 'How to lose weight permanently – without dieting'. Orbach offers a psychoanalytic approach heavily informed by the Women's Liberation Movement. She rejects the traditional Freudian interpretation, which reduced overeating and obesity to character defects, and argues instead that they should be 'perceived as the expression of painful and conflicting experiences'. Compulsive eating, she argues, is rooted in the social inequality of women: 'Fat is a social disease', consciously or unconsciously 'a challenge to sex-role stereotyping and culturally defined experience of womanhood.'

6. P. Garfinkel, K. Halmi and B. Shaw, 'Applications of Current Research Findings to Treatment: What We Need for the Future,' in G. H. Anderson, and S. Kennedy, (eds), *The Biology of Feast and Famine: Relevance to Eating Disorders*, San Diego, CA: Academic Press, 1992, pp. 370–85.

7. J. Garrow, *Treat Obesity Seriously*, Edinburgh: Churchill Livingstone, 1981.

8. B. Donovan, *Hormones and Human Behaviour*, Cambridge: Cambridge University Press, 1985.

A variant of the set-point theory that held sway for a time conjured up a medical variant of the insatiable inner force. Jules Hirsch, a leading obesity researcher at the Rockefeller University in New York, argued that people who become obese before the age of twenty or so tend to develop more fat cells than normal, and are then stuck with this number for life. Hirsch speculated that in the ex-obese individual these numerous – but now shrunken – cells cry out to be filled with fats. He argued that they might produce some chemical signal, perhaps some sort of hormone, that would stimulate the desire to eat. In his view, thin adults who had been fat children would 'naturally' reach a higher body weight if they responded to the incessant demands of their too-numerous fat cells. It is an appealing idea, but one for which there is little evidence. Despite years of trying, no one has found any hormone or neural connection that might relate the status of an individual's fat cells to their food consumption.

9. V. Tarasuk and G. Beaton, 'The Nature and Individuality of Within-Subject Variation in Energy Intake,' *American Journal of Clinical Nutrition* 54 (1991): 464–70.
10. Garrow, *Treat Obesity Seriously*.
11. A. Stunkard and T. Wadden, 'Psychological Aspects of Human Obesity', in *Obesity*, Philadelphia: J.B. Lippincott, 1992, pp. 352–60.
12. S. Mennell, *All Manners of Food: Eating and Taste in England and France from the Middle Ages to the Present*, Oxford: Basil Blackwell, 1985; S. Mennell, 'On the Civilising of Appetite', *Theory, Culture and Society* 4 (1987): 373–403; M. Rintala and P. Mustajoki, 'Could Mannequins Menstruate?', *British Medical Journal* 305 (1992): 1575–6.
13. P. Rogers, 'Fat is a Fictional Issue: The Novel and the Rise of Weight-Watching', in M. Mulvey Roberts and R. Porter (eds), *Literature and Medicine During the Eighteenth Century*, London: Routledge, 1993.
14. E.J. Button and A. Whitehouse, 'Subclinical Anorexia Nervosa', *Psychological Medicine* 11 (1991): 509–16.
15. C. Manser, *The Assessment of Stress in Laboratory Animals*, Horsham, Sussex: RSPCA (1992).
16. W.B. Cannon, *The Wisdom of the Body*, New York: W.W. Norton and Co. Inc., 1939.
17. H. Selye, *The Stress of Life*, New York: McGraw-Hill, 1976.
18. R. Sapolsky, 'Neuroendocrinology of the Stress-Response', in J. Becker, S.M. Breedlove, and D. Crews (eds), *Behavioral Endocrinology*, Cambridge, MA: MIT Press, 1992, pp. 287–324.
19. S. Levine, C. Coe and S. Wiener, 'Psychoneuroendocrinology of Stress: A Psychobiological Perspective', in F.R. Brush, and S. Levine (eds), *Psychoendocrinology*, San Diego, CA: Academic Press, 1989.
20. The Coronary Prevention Group, proceedings of a conference, 'Does Stress Cause Heart Attacks? Psychosocial Factors in CHD', London, 18–19 November 1985.
21. S. Lyng, 'Edgework: A Social Psychological Analysis of Voluntary Risk Taking', *American Journal of Sociology* 95 (1990): 882–90.

22. J. Hanmer and J. Hearn, 'Gendered Research and Researching Gender: Women, Men and Violence', British Sociological Association Conference, University of Essex, 5–8 April 1993.

23. J. Jones, 'Beat Stress to Boost Beauty', *BBC Good Health*, March 1993: 70–72.

24. S. Shuttleworth, 'Patriarchal Science', *Science as Culture* 2 (1991): 12.

25. S. Shuttleworth, 'Ideologies of Bourgeois Motherhood in the Mid-Victorian Era', in L. Shires (ed.), *Rewriting the Victorians*, London: Routledge, 1992.

26. A. Hochschild, *The Managed Heart: Commercialization of Human Feeling*, Berkeley, CA: University of California Press, 1983.

27. A. Lubell, 'Does Steroid Abuse Cause – Or Excuse – Violence?', *The Physician and Sportsmedicine* 17 (1989): 176–85.

28. Hitler's final days recalled by physician, *American Medical News*, 11 October 1985: 1.

29. M.S. Bahrke, C.E. Yesalis and J.E. Wright, 'Psychological and Behavioral Effects of Endogenous Testosterone Levels and Anabolic-Androgenic Steroids among Males: A Review', *Sports Medicine* 10 (1990): 303–37; P. Pallot, 'Steroids Can Turn Athletes Into Killers', *Daily Telegraph*, 29 May 1993.

30. F. Huntingford, 'Animals Fight, But Do Not Make War', in J. Groebel and R. Hinde (eds), *Aggression and War: Their Biological and Social Bases*, Cambridge: Cambridge University Press, 1989, pp. 25–34.

31. C.E. Yesalis, J.E. Wright and J.A. Lombardo, 'Anabolic-Androgenic Steroids: A Synthesis of Existing Data and Recommendations for Future Research', *Clinical Sports Medicine* 1 (1989): 109–34.

32. R. Langevin, (1991) 'Biological and Psychological Factors in Human Aggression', in M. Haug, P.F. Brain and C. Aron (eds), *Heterotypical Behaviour in Man and Animals*, London: Chapman & Hall, pp. 195–214.

33. R. Blow, 'A Social Disease', *Mother Jones*, May/June 1993: 26–8.

34. J.M.R. Delgado, *Physical Control of the Mind*, New York: Harper & Row, 1969.

35. Langevin, 'Biological and Psychological Factors'.

36. B. Eichelman, 'Neurochemical and Psychopharmacologic Aspects of Aggressive Behavior', *Annual Reviews of Medicine* 41 (1990): 149–58.

37. J. Herbert, (1989) 'The Physiology of Aggression', in Groebel and Hinde (eds), *Aggression and War*, pp. 58–74.

38. J.H. Goldstein, (1989) 'Beliefs about Human Aggression', in Groebel and Hinde (eds), *Aggression and War*, pp. 10–22.

39. Hochschild, *The Managed Heart*.

40. R.C. Simons and C.C. Hughes (eds), *The Culture-bound Syndromes: Folk Illnesses of Psychiatric and Anthropological Interest*, Dordrecht, Holland: D. Reidel, 1985.

41. D. Denno, *Biology and Violence: From Birth to Adulthood*, Cambridge: Cambridge University Press, 1990.

42. B. Greenstein, *The Fragile Male*, London: Boxtree, 1993.

43. D. Sexton, 'Why All Men Really Are Rats', *Sunday Telegraph*, 30 May 1993, p. 16.

44. M. Marrin, 'Why Annie Oakley Was Firing Blanks', *The Sunday Telegraph*, 8 November 1992, p. 11.

45. C. Shilling, *The Body and Social Theory*, London: Sage, 1993.

46. P. Freund, 'Understanding Socialized Human Nature', *Theory and Society* 17 (1988): 839–64; P. Freund, 'The Expressive Body: A Common Ground for the Sociology of Emotions and Health and Illness', *Sociology of Health and Illness* 12 (1990): 454–77; P. Freund and M. McGuire, *Health, Illness and the Social Body*, Englewood Cliffs, NJ: Prentice Hall, 1991.

47. R. Shepherd, 'Talking Up a Storm', *The Sunday Times Magazine*, 16 May 1993, pp. 46–50; P. Rodenburg, *The Need for Words*, London: Methuen, 1993.

48. F. Huntingford and A. Turner, 'Aggression: A Biological Imperative?', *New Scientist*, 4 August 1988: 44–7.

4: Hormones on the Brain

1. S. Freud, 'Femininity', in J. Strachey (ed.), *New Introductory Lectures on Psycho-Analysis*, London: Hogarth, 1933.

2. The pink/blue switch-round is reported by S. Salmans, 'Objects and Gender: When an It Evolves into a He or a She', *New York Times*, 16 November 1989, B1. Salmans reports the work of Jo Paoletti, who offers no explanation for the colour swap. See J.B. Paoletti and C.L. Kregloh, 'The Children's Department', in C. Brush Kidwell and V. Steel (eds), *Men and Women: Dressing the Part*, Washington, DC: Smithsonian Institution Press, 1989. Quoted in M. Garber, *Vested Interests: Cross-Dressing and Cultural Anxiety*, Harmondsworth: Penguin, 1992.

3. C.H. Phoenix, R.W. Goy, A.A. Gerall, and W.C. Young, 'Organizing Action of Prenatally Administered Testosterone Proprionate on the Tissues Mediating Mating Behavior in the Female Guinea Pig', *Endocrinology* 65 (1959): 369–82. See also M. Van den Wijngaard, 'The Acceptance of Scientific Theories and Images of Masculinity and Femininity 1959–1985', *Journal of the History of Biology* 24 (1991): 19–49. John Money argues that in fact Eugen Steinach was the first to demonstrate, in the early years of the twentieth century, that the mating behaviour of female guinea pigs could be masculinised by castrating them soon after birth and implanting testicular tissue. 'The theoretical implications of Steinach's findings were too advanced for the time and lay dormant until William Young confirmed the experiment in the 1950s,' Money writes ('Agenda and Credenda of the Kinsey Scale', in D. McWhirter *et al.* [eds], *Homosexuality/Heterosexuality*, Oxford: Oxford University Press, 1990, pp. 41–60). See also E. Steinach, *Sex and Life: Forty Years of Biological and Medical Experiments*, New York: Viking, 1940.

4. J. Weeks, 'Introduction', *Seminars in the Neurosciences* 3 (1991): 435–6; A.P. Arnold and S.M. Breedlove, 'Organisational and Activational Effects of Sex Steroids On the Brain and Behavior: a Reanalysis', *Hormones and Behavior* 19 (1985): 469–98.
5. C.H. Hsu and C.S. Carter, 'Social Isolation Inhibits Male-Like Sexual Behaviour in Female Hamsters', *Behavioral and Neural Biology* 46 (1986): 242–7; R. Whalen, 'Heterotypical Behaviour in Man and Animals: Concepts and Strategies', in M. Haug, P.F. Brain and C. Aron (eds), *Heterotypical Behaviour in Man and Animals*, London: Chapman & Hall, 1991, p. 218.
6. G. Morali and C. Beyer, 'Motor Aspects of Masculine Sexual Behaviour in Rats and Rabbits', *Advances in the Study of Behavior* 21 (1992): 201–38, London: Academic Press.
7. C.L. Moore and G.A. Morelli, 'Mother Rats Interact Differently with Male and Female Offspring', *Journal of Comparative and Physiological Psychology* 93 (1979): 677–84; C.L. Moore, 'Maternal Behaviour of Rats Is Affected by Hormonal Condition of Pups', *Journal of Comparative and Physiological Psychology* 96 (1982): 123–9; C.L. Moore, H. Dou, and J.M. Juraska, 'Maternal Stimulation Affects the Number of Motor Neurons in a Sexually Dimorphic Nucleus of the Lumbar Spinal Cord', *Brain Research* 572 (1992): 52–6.
8. S. LeVay, *The Sexual Brain*, Cambridge, MA: MIT Press, 1993.
9. F.A. Beach, 'The Snark was a Boojum', *American Psychology* 5 (1950): 115–24; F.A. Beach, 'Animal Models of Human Sexuality', in *Sex, Hormones and Behaviour*, Ciba Foundation Symposium No. 62, Excerpta Medica, 1979, pp. 113–43.
10. G. O'Neill, 'Sex on the Brain', *Melbourne Age*, 21 October 1992, p. 11, cited in L. Rogers, 'Sex Differences in Cognition: The New Rise of Biologism', *The Australian Educational and Developmental Psychologist*, 10 (1992): 37–49.
11. M. Holloway, 'Profile: Vive la Différence', *Scientific American*, October 1990: 16–17.
12. E. Hampson and D. Kimura, 'Sex Differences and Hormonal Influences on Cognitive Function in Humans', in J. Becker, S.M. Breedlove and D. Crews (eds), *Behavioral Endocrinology*, Cambridge, MA: MIT Press, 1992, pp. 357–400; D. Kimura, 'Sex Differences in the Brain', *Scientific American* 267 (1992): 81–7.
13. V.J. Shute, J.W. Pellegrino, L. Hurbert and R.W. Reynolds, 'The Relationship Between Androgen Levels and Human Spatial Abilities', *Bulletin of the Psychonomic Society* 21 (1983): 465–8.
14. C. Gouchie and D. Kimura, 'The Relationship between Testosterone Levels and Cognitive Ability Patterns', *Psychoneuroendocrinology* 16 (1991): 323–34.
15. P.J. Peters, P. Servos and R. Day, 'Marked Sex Differences on a Fine Motor Skill Task Disappear When Finger Size Is Used as a Covariate', *Journal of Applied Psychology*, 75 (1990): 87–90; H. Fisher, *Anatomy of Love: The Natural History of Monogamy, Adultery and Divorce*, New York: Simon & Schuster, 1993.

16. P. Caplan, G. Macpherson and P. Tobin, 'Do Sex-Related Differences in Spatial Abilities Exist?', *American Psychologist* 40 (1985): 786–99.
17. A. Feingold, 'Cognitive Gender Differences Are Disappearing', *American Psychologist* 43 (1988): 95–103; J.S. Hyde and M.C. Linn, 'Gender Differences in Verbal Ability: a Meta-analysis', *Psychological Bulletin* 104 (1988): 53–69.
18. S. Jay Gould, *The Mismeasure of Man*, New York: W.W. Norton, 1981.
19. J. Archer and B. Lloyd, *Sex and Gender*, Cambridge: Cambridge University Press, 1985; B. Davies, *Frogs and Snails and Feminist Tales*, North Sydney: Allen & Unwin, 1989.
20. R. Hubbard, *The Politics of Women's Biology*, New Brunswick: Rutgers University Press, 1990, pp. 115–16.
21. D. Kimura, 'Sex Differences, Human Brain Organisation', in G. Adelman (ed.), *Encyclopedia of Neuroscience*, Boston, MA: Birkhauser, 1987, pp. 1084–5.
22. D.F. Swaab and E. Fliers, 'A Sexually Dimorphic Nucleus in the Human Brain', *Science* 228 (1985): 1112–15; D.F. Swaab, M.A. Hofman and B. Fisser, 'Sexual Differentiation of the Human Brain,' *Neuroendocrinology Letters* 10 (1988): 222.
23. D. Kelly, 'Sexual Differentiation of the Nervous System', in E. Kandel *et al.*, *Principles of Neural Science*, 3rd edn, Amsterdam: Elsevier, 1991.
24. E. Baulieu, 'Preface', in Haug, Brain and Aron (eds), *Heterotypical Behaviour in Man and Animals*.
25. H.F.L. Meyer-Bahlburg, 'Psychoendocrine Research on Sexual Orientation: Current Status and Future Options', *Progress in Brain Research* 61 (1984): 375–98; A. Ehrhardt, R. Epstein and J. Money, 'Fetal Androgens and Female Gender Identity in the Early-Treated Androgenital Syndrome', *Johns Hopkins Medical Journal* 122 (1968): 160–67; A.A. Ehrhardt, K. Evers and J. Money, 'Influence of Androgen and Some Aspects of Sexually Dimorphic Behavior in Women with Late-Treated Adrenogenital Syndrome', *Johns Hopkins Medical Journal* 123 (1968): 115–22.
26. J. Money and A.A. Ehrhardt, *Man and Woman, Boy and Girl: The Differentiation and Dimorphism of Gender Identity from Conception to Maturity*, Baltimore, MD: Johns Hopkins University Press, 1972; J. Money, M. Schwartz and V.G. Lewis, 'Adult Heterosexual Status and Fetal Hormonal Masculinization and Demasculinization: 46XX Congenital Virilizing Adrenal Hyperplasia and 46XY Androgen Insensitivity Syndrome Compared', *Psychoneuroendocrinology* 9 (1984): 405–14; J. Money, *Gay, Straight and In-Between*, Oxford: Oxford University Press, 1988.
27. R.M. Mulaikal, C.J. Migeon and J.A. Rock, 'Fertility Rates in Female Patients with Congenital Adrenal Hyperplasia Due to 21-Hydroxylase Deficiency', *New England Journal of Medicine* 316 (1987): 178–82.
28. F. Slijper, 'Androgens and Gender Role Behavior in Girls with Congenital Adrenal Hyperplasia (CAH)', in G.J. De Vries, J.P.C. De Bruin *et al.*,

(eds), *Progress in Brain Research* vol. 61, *Sex Differences in the Brain*, Amsterdam: Elsevier, 1984, pp. 417–22.

29. R. Bleier, (1986) 'Sex Differences Research: Science or Belief?', in Ruth Bleier (ed.), *Feminist Approaches to Science*, Oxford: Pergamon, pp. 147–64.

30. R. Whalen, D. Geary and F. Johnson, 'Models of Sexuality', in D. McWhirter, S. Sanders and J. Machover Reinisch (eds), *Homosexuality/Heterosexuality: Concepts of Sexual Orientation*, Oxford: Oxford University Press, 1990, pp. 61–70.

31. J. Imperato-McGinley and R.E. Peterson, 'Male Pseudohermaphroditism: The Complexities of Male Phenotypic Development', *American Journal of Medicine* 61 (1976): 251–72; J. Imperato-McGinley, R.E. Peterson, T. Gautier and E. Sturla, 'Androgens and the Evolution of Male-Gender Identity among Male Pseudohermaphrodites with 5-alpha-reductase Deficiency', *New England Journal of Medicine* 300 (1979): 1233–7.

32. S. LeVay, *The Sexual Brain*, Cambridge, MA: MIT Press, 1993.

33. J. Imperato-McGinley, M. Miller, J.D. Wilson, R.E. Peterson, C. Shackleton and D.C. Gajdusek, 'A Cluster of Male Pseudohermaphrodites with 5-alpha-reductase Deficiency in Papua New Guinea', *Clinical Endocrinology* 34 (1991): 293–8.

34. A. Fausto-Sterling, *Myths of Gender*, revised edn, New York: Basic Books, 1992.

35. H. Meyer-Bahlburg, A.A. Ehrhardt, L. Rosen, J. Feldman, N. Veridiano, I. Zimmerman and B. McEwen, 'Psychosexual Milestones in Women Prenatally Exposed to Diethylstilbestrol', *Hormones and Behavior* 18 (1984): 359–66.

36. J.M. Reinisch, M. Ziemba-Davis and S.A. Sanders, 'Hormonal Contributions to Sexually Dimorphic Behavioral Development in Humans', *Psychoneuroendocrinology* 16 (1991): 213–78.

37. A.A. Ehrhardt and J. Money, 'Progestin-induced Hermaphroditism: IQ and Psychosexual Identity in a Study of Ten Girls', *Journal of Sex Research* 3 (1967): 83–100; L.S. McGuire and G.S. Omenn, 'Congenital Adrenal Hyperplasia in Family Studies of IQ', *Behavioral Genetics* 5 (1975): 165–73.

38. E. Hampson and D. Kimura, 'Sex Differences and Hormonal Influences on Cognitive Function in Humans,' in J.B. Becker *et al.*, *Behavioral Endocrinology*, Cambridge, MA: MIT Press, 1992, pp. 357–98.

39. J.M. Reinisch, M. Ziemba-Davis and S. Sanders, 'Hormonal Contributions to Sexually Dimorphic Behavioral Development in Humans,' *Psychoneuroendocrinology* 16 (1991): 213–78.

40. R. Sharpe and N. Skakkebaek, 'Are Oestregens Involved in Falling Sperm Counts and Disorders of the Male Reproductive Tract?' *The Lancet*, 341 (1993): 1392–5.

41. The comments come, respectively, from Niels Skakkebaek, John McLachlan, scientific director of the National Institute of Environmental Health Sciences in Research, Triangle Park, North Carolina, and Richard Sharpe, personal communications.

42. S. Kessler, 'The Medical Construction of Gender: Case Management of

Intersexed Infants', *Signs* 16 (1990): 3–26.

43. G. Vines, 'Last Olympics For the Sex Test?', *New Scientist*, 4 July 1992: 39–42.

44. J. Money, *Gay, Straight and In-Between*, Oxford: Oxford University Press, 1988.

45. H. Longino, *Science as Social Knowledge*, Princeton, NJ: Princeton University Press, 1990.

46. L. Birke, *Women, Feminism and Biology*, Brighton: Harvester, 1986.

47. *The Pink Paper*, London, 16 May 1993, p. 5.

48. S. Witelson, 'Neural Sexual Mosaicism: Sexual Differentiation of the Human Temporo-Parietal Region for Functional Asymmetry', *Psychoneuroendocrinology* 16 (1991): 131–54.

49. E. Showalter, *Sexual Anarchy*, London: Bloomsbury, 1991.

50. For example, S.J. Glass, H.J. Deuel and C.A. Wright, 'Sex Hormone Studies in Male Homosexuality', *Endocrinology* 26 (1940): 590–94. In 1971, researchers reported that a group of predominantly homosexual men had lower testosterone levels than the heterosexual controls. Scientific colleagues later pointed to methodological flaws – many of the homosexual group were habitual marijuana smokers – which is now known to reduce testosterone levels – and four were not producing sperm and apparently had testicular disease: R.C. Kolodny, W.H. Masters, J. Hendryx and G. Toro, 'Plasma Testosterone and Semen Analysis in Male Homosexuals', *New England Journal of Medicine* 285 (1971): 1170–74.

51. J. Bancroft, *Human Sexuality and Its Problems*, 2nd edn, Edinburgh: Churchill Livingstone, 1989.

52. F.E. Kenyon, 'Physique and Physical Health of Female Homosexuals', *Journal of Neurology and Neurosurgical Psychiatry* 31 (1968): 487–9. See also M.W. Perkins, 'Female Homosexuality and Body Build', *Archives of Sexual Behavior* 10 (1981): 337–45.

53. J. Downey, A. Ehrhardt, M. Schiffman, I. Dyrenfurth and J. Becker, 'Sex Hormones in Lesbian and Heterosexual Women', *Hormones and Behavior* 21 (1987): 347–57.

54. G. Dörner, W. Rohde, G. Schott and C. Schabel, 'On the LH Response to Oestrogen and LHRH in Transsexual Men', *Experimental Clinical Endocrinology* 82 (1983): 257–67; G. Dörner *et al.*, 'Sexual Differentiation of Gonadotrophin Secretion, Sexual Orientation and Gender Role Behavior', *Journal of Steroid Biochemistry* 27 (1987): 1081–7.

55. L. Gooren, 'The Endocrinology of Transsexualism: A Review and Commentary', *Psychoneuroendocrinology* 15 (1990): 3–14.

Based on his studies of transsexuals, Louis Gooren also argues that not only is it wrong to equate human sexuality with animal couplings, but it is a mistake to equate human sexuality with having babies or even having sex. Physically, transsexuals are demonstrably 'normal' men and women, and have often established conventional heterosexual relationships. Yet, by definition, they think of themselves as trapped in a body of the wrong sex. Something as complex as this experience, says Gooren, depends on our sophisticated mental life. And focusing on transsexuals' 'reproductive behaviour' reveals nothing about their condition: some male-to-female transsexuals are erotically attracted to women, have sex with them and father children. Similarly, many female-to-male transsexuals are sexually attracted to men, and are mothers. 'Observation of their sexual performance would provide no clue about their gender dysphoria,' he says.

Transsexual surgery has been performed since 1922, but it became much more common after the Christine Jorgensen case made headlines in 1953. Jan (formerly James) Morris argues in her autobiography *Conundrum* (New York: Henry Holt, 1974; 1986) that the era of transsexuality has passed; fewer individuals will seek these operations, she predicts, because cultural changes may have lessened the need to seek surgical solutions to their gender dysphoria.

Nonetheless, researchers continue to search for biological differences between transsexuals and non-transsexuals. Simon LeVay is convinced that 'gender identity' – which he defines as 'the subjective sense of one's own sex' – cannot be put down to 'life experiences' (*The Sexual Brain*, Cambridge, MA: MIT Press, 1993). 'I feel confident that biological markers for transsexuality will eventually be identified,' writes LeVay. This, he believes, will provide insights into 'the developmental mechanisms' that create gender identity.

56. G. Dörner and G. Hinz, 'Induction and Prevention of Male Homosexuality by Androgen', *Journal of Endocrinology* 40 (1968): 387–8.
57. C. Manser, *The Assessment of Stress in Laboratory Animals*, London: Royal Society for the Prevention of Cruelty to Animals, 1992.
58. S. LeVay, *The Sexual Brain*, Cambridge, MA: MIT Press, 1993.
59. W. Ricketts, 'Biological Research on Homosexuality: Ansell's Cow or Occam's Razor?', in J. P. De Cecco (ed.), *Gay Personality and Sexual Labelling*, Harrington Park Press, 1985, pp. 65–93. See also L. Birke, 'Is Homosexuality Hormonally Determined?', *Journal of Homosexuality* 6 (1981): 35–49.
60. R. Whalen, D. Geary and F. Johnson, 'Models of Sexuality'.
61. C. Hooper, 'Biology, Brain Architecture and Human Sexuality', *National Institutes of Health Newsletter* 4 (1992): 54.
62. S. LeVay, 'A Difference in Hypothalamic Structure between Heterosexual and Homosexual Men', *Science* 253 (1991): 1034.
63. L.S. Allen, M. Hines, J.E. Shryne and R.A. Gorski, 'Two Sexually Dimorphic Cell Groups in the Human Brain', *Journal of Neuroscience* 9 (1989): 497.
64. J. Maddox,' Is Homosexuality Hard-Wired?' *Nature* 353 (1991): 13.
65. D.F. Swaab, Lecture: 'The Human Hypothalamus in Relation to Gender and Sexual Orientation', 19 November 1992 at AFRC Institute of Animal Physiology and Genetics Research, Cambridge Research Station, Babraham.
66. D.F. Swaab and M.A. Hofman, *Brain Research* 537 (1990): 141.

67. L.S. Allen, M.F. Richey, Y.M. Chai and R.A. Gorski, 'Sex Differences in the Corpus Callosum of the Living Human Being', *Journal of Neuroscience* 11 (1991): 933–42.

68. A. Fausto-Sterling, 'Why Do We Know So Little About Human Sex?', *Discover*, June 1992: 28–30.

69. E. Marshall, 'Sex on the Brain', *Science* 257 (1992): 620.

70. D. Gelman *et al.*, 'Born or Bred?', *Newsweek*, 24 February 1992: 41.

71. S. LeVay, *The Sexual Brain*.

72. S. LeVay, 'Are Homosexuals Born and Not Made?', *The Guardian*, 9 October 1992, p. 31.

73. R.C. Pillard and J.D. Weinrich, 'The Periodic Table Model of the Gender Transpositions: Part I, A Theory Based on Masculinisation and Defeminisation of the Brain', *Journal of Sex Research* 23 (1987): 425–54; J. Kirsch and J. Weinrich, 'Homosexuality, Nature, and Biology: Is Homosexuality Natural? Does it Matter?', in J. Gonsiorek and J. Weinrich (eds), *Homosexuality: Research Implications for Public Policy*, London: Sage, 1991, pp. 13–31.

74. J.M. Bailey and R.C. Pillard, 'A Genetic Study of Male Sexual Orientation', *Archives of General Psychiatry* 48 (1991): 1089–96.

75. J.M. Bailey, R.C. Pillard and Y. Agyei, 'A Genetic Study of Female Sexual Orientation', *Archives of General Psychiatry* (1993) (in press); and B. Bower, 'Genetic Clues to Female Homosexuality', *Science News* 142 (1992): 117.

76. Gelman *et al.*, 'Born or Bred?'.

77. J. Eckersley, 'The Secret I Wish They'd Never Told me', *Living*, March 1993: pp. 75–7.

78. C. Silverstein, 'Psychological and Medical Treatments of Homosexuality', in Gonsiorek and Weinrich (eds), *Homosexuality: Research Implications for Public Policy*, pp. 101–14.

79. G. Schmidt, 'Allies and Persecutors: Science and Medicine in the Homosexual Issue', *Journal of Homosexuality* 10 (1984): 127–40.

80. L. Rieber and V. Sigusch, 'Psychosurgery in Sex Offenders and Sexual "Deviants" in West Germany', *Archives of Sexual Behaviour* 8 (1979): 523–7.

81. Dörner and Hinz, 'Induction and Prevention of Male Homosexuality by Androgen', F. Gotz, W. Rohde and G. Dörner, 'Neuroendocrine Differentiation of Sex-Specific Gonadotrophin Secretion, Sexual Orientation and Gender Role Behaviour', in M. Haug, P.F. Brain and C. Aron (eds), *Heterotypical Behavior in Man and Animals*, pp. 167–94. See also V. Sigusch, E. Schorsch, M. Dannecker and G. Schmidt, 'Official Statement by the German Society for Sex Research On the Research of Professor Dr Günter Dörner on the Subject of Homosexuality', *Archives of Sexual Behaviour* 11 (1982): 445–9.

82. Reinisch, Ziemba-Davis and Sanders, 'Hormonal Contributions to Sexually Dimorphic Behavioral Development in Humans'.

83. D. Kimura, 'Sex Differences in the Brain'.

84. A. Fausto-Sterling, *Myths of Gender*, revised edn, New York: Basic Books, 1992.

In a recent study of male stewards on aeroplanes, Albert Mills of Athabasca University in Canada argued that 'men in a now predominantly female occupation have brought confusion to some in an industry known for its sharp heterosexual images of masculinity and femininity'. A BBC documentary on flight attendants in 1991 implied that stewards were typically gay ('associated with gentleness and caring'), on the grounds that the men had joined a predominantly female profession. There is evidence, Mills said, that homophobic attitudes run deep in the industry. In 1987 a Canadian steward was fired for wearing an earring, regarded as a sign of homosexuality: 'Strategy, Sexuality and the Stratosphere: Airlines and the Gendering of Organisation', British Sociological Association Conference, University of Essex, 5–8 April 1993.

85. Silverstein, 'Psychological and Medical Treatments of Homosexuality'.
86. J. Gagnon, 'Gender Preference in Erotic Relations', in J. McWhirter *et al.*, *Homosexuality/Heterosexuality: Concepts of Sexual Orientation*, Oxford: Oxford University Press, 1990, pp. 176–207.
87. J. Money, 'Agenda and Credenda of the Kinsey Scale', in ibid., pp. 41–60.
88. Silverstein, 'Psychological and Medical Treatments of Homosexuality'.
89. D. Gelman *et al.*, 'Born or Bred?', *Newsweek*, 24 February 1992: 38–44.
90. G. Herdt, 'Developmental Discontinuities and Sexual Orientation Across Cultures', in McWhirter *et al.*, *Homosexuality/Heterosexuality*, pp. 212–35.
91. P. Blumstein and P. Schwartz, 'Intimate Relationships and the Creation of Sexuality', in ibid., pp. 307–35.
92. S. Lipsitz Bem, 'On the Inadequacy of Our Sexual Categories: A Personal Perspective', in S. Wilkinson and C. Kitzinger (eds), *Heterosexuality*, London: Sage, 1993; S. Bem, *The Lenses of Gender: Transforming the Debate on Sexual Inequality*, New Haven, CT: Yale University Press, 1993.
93. Ruth Wallsgrove, personal communication, 1993.
94. D. Swaab, Lecture: 'The Human Hypothalamus in Relation to Gender and Sexual Orientation'.

5: Time for Hormones?

1. R. Wilson, *Feminine Forever*, New York: M. Evans, 1966.
2. F. McCrea, 'The Politics of Menopause: The "Discovery" of a Deficiency Disease', *Social Problems* 31 (1983): 111–23.
3. R.A. Wilson and T.A. Wilson, 'The Fate of the Non-Treated Postmenopausal Woman: A Plea for Maintenance of Adequate Estrogen from Puberty to the Grave', *Journal of the American Geriatrics Society* 11 (1963): 347–62.
4. R.A. Wilson and T.A. Wilson, 'The Basic Philosophy of Estrogen Maintenance', *Journal of the American Geriatrics Society* 20 (1972): 521–3.
5. G. Sheehy, *The Silent Passage*, London: Harper Collins, 1993.
6. K. Hawkes, J. O'Connell and N. Blurton Jones, 'Hardworking Hadza Grandmothers', in V. Standen and R.A. Foley (eds), *Comparative Socioecology: The Behavioural Ecology of Humans and Other Mammals*, Oxford: Blackwell, 1989, pp. 341–66.

7. S. Washburn, 'Longevity in primates', in J. March and J. McGaugh (eds), *Aging, Biology and Behaviour*, New York: Academic Press, 1981, pp. 11–29.

8. J. Stevenson, 'New Treatments for Osteoporosis', lecture at Society for Endocrinology meeting, Royal Society of Medicine, London, 27 November 1992.

9. D. Nelkin, *Selling Science*, New York: W.H. Freeman, 1987.

10. F. McCrea and G. Markle, 'The Estrogen Replacement Controversy in the USA and the UK: Different Answers to the Same Question?', *Social Studies of Science* 14 (1984): 1–26.

11. J. Studd and M. Thom, 'Letter to the Editor', *New England Journal of Medicine* 300 (1979): 922–3.

12. D. Purdie *et al.*, 'Some Observations on the Densitometric Screening of a Perimenopausal Population', *Journal of Endocrinology*, 135 (supplement) (1992): 014.

13. Stevenson, 'New Treatments for Osteoporosis'.

14. P. Kaufert and S. McKinlay, 'Estrogen-Replacement Therapy: The Production of Medical Knowledge and the Emergence of Policy', in E. Lewin and V. Olesen (eds), *Women, Health and Healing*, New York: Tavistock, 1985.

15. K. T. Khaw, 'The Menopause and Hormone Replacement Therapy', *Postgraduate Medical Journal* 68 (1992): 615–23.

16. Stevenson, 'New Treatments for Osteoporosis'.

17. G. Greer, *The Change*, Harmondsworth; Penguin, 1992.

18. M. Lock, P. Kaufert and P. Gilbert, 'Cultural Construction of the Menopausal Syndrome: The Japanese Case', *Maturitas* 10 (1988) : 317–22; P. Kaufert and M. Lock, '"What Are Women For?" Cultural Constructions of Menopausal Women in Japan and Canada', in V. Kerns and J. Brown (eds), *In Her Prime*, 2nd edn, Urbana, IL: University of Illinois Press, 1992, pp. 201–20; M. Lock, *Encounters with Aging: Mythologies of Menopause in Japan and North America*, Berkeley and Los Angeles: University of California Press, 1993.

19. *British Medical Journal*, vol. 303; 1991, 1354: 'Fats Less Dangerous to Women', *The Independent*, 21 March 1992.

20. *Wall Street Journal*, 9 September 1992; *Time*, 9 November 1992; *Circulation*, 8 September 1992.

21. C. Cooper and R. Eastell, 'Bone Gain and Loss in Premenopausal Women', *British Medical Journal*, 306 (1993): 1357–8. M. Notelovitz, 'Osteoporosis: Screening, Prevention and Management', *Fertility and Sterility*, 59 (1993): 707–25.

22. J. Zhang *et al.*, 'Moderate Physical Activity and Bone Density among Perimenopausal Women', *American Journal of Public Health* (1992) 82: 736–8.

23. H. Adlercreutz, 'Diet, Breast Cancer, and Sex Hormone Metabolism', *Annals of the New York Academy of Sciences*; 595 (1990): 281–90.

24. Anon., *International Herald Tribune*, 29 February–1 March 1992.

25. S. Bewley and T.H. Bewley, 'Drug Dependence with Oestrogen Replacement Therapy', *The Lancet* 339 (1992): 290–91.

NOTES

26. J. Studd, Letter in *The Times*, 6 February 1992.

27. R.M. Francis, *et al.*, 'Male Osteoporosis', *Journal of Endocrinology* 135 (supplement) (1992): 015.

28. S. Langan, 'Male Menopause? Take a Pill', *The Sunday Times*, 28 June 1992, section 5, p. 1; in contrast, Gail Sheehy argues the case for the male menopause in 'The Unspeakable Passage – Is There a Male Menopause?', *Vanity Fair*, March 1993.

29. A. Riley, 'The Ageing Testis', *British Journal of Sexual Medicine*, December 1987: 325–6.

30. C. Hall, 'Caution Urged On Hormone Therapy', *The Independent*, 3 June 1993.

31. J. LeFanu, 'Testosterone: Cure or Tonic?' *The Sunday Telegraph*, 21 March 1993.

32. Stevenson, 'New Treatments for Osteoporosis'.

33. F. Weldon, *Life Force*, London: HarperCollins, 1992.

34. M. Flint (1982) 'Male and Female Menopause: A Cultural Put-on', in A. Voda *et al.* (eds), *Changing Perspectives on Menopause*, Austin, TX: University of Texas Press, 1982, pp. 363–78.

35. Y. Beyene, *From Menarche to Menopause: Reproductive Lives of Peasant Women in Two Cultures*, Albany, NY: State University of New York Press, 1989; 'Menopause', *Newsweek*, 25 May 1992: 39–44.

36. J. Lancaster and B. King, 'An Evolutionary Perspective on Menopause', in Kerns and J. Brown (eds), *In Her Prime*.

37. E. Martin, *The Woman in the Body: A Cultural Analysis of Reproduction*, Boston, MA: Beacon Press, 1987.

38. M. Lock, 'Contested Meanings of the Menopause', *The Lancet*, 337 (1991): 1270–72.

39. McCrea and Markle, 'The Estrogen Replacement Controversy'.

40. Fielding, 'Farewell, Witchy Woman', *The Sunday Times*, 24 May 1992.

41. Wendy Cooper, *No Change: A Biological Revolution for Women*, London: Hutchinson, 1975.

42. Fielding, 'Farewell, Witchy Woman'.

43. Sheehy, *The Silent Passage*.

44. Jane Lewis, 'Feminism, the Menopause and Hormone Replacement', *Feminist Review* 43 (1993): 38–56.

45. John Woodward, 'Leave HRT Choice Up To the Patient', *GP*, 27 January 1989. Two leading gynaecologists also advise their colleagues: 'Asymptomatic women without risk factors for osteoporosis should make their own decisions about hormone replacement therapy after being given up-to-date information about risks and benefits.' H.S. Jacobs and F.E. Loeffler, 'Postmenopausal Hormone Replacement Therapy', *British Medical Journal*, 305 (1992): 1403–8.

46. P. Kaufert, 'Myth and the Menopause', *Sociology of Health and Illness* 4 (1982): 141–66.

47. Lewis, 'Feminism, the Menopause and Hormone Replacement'.

48. T. Powles, 'On Trial: Drugs That May Prevent Disease,' *New Scientist*, 19 January 1991, p. 16.

49. Two commentators expressed concern, however: see A. Oakley, 'Tamoxifen: In Whose Best Interest?' *New Scientist*, 22 June 1991, p. 12. Carolyn Faulder, 'Better Safe Than Sorry', *Bulletin of Medical Ethics*, 75 (Jan/Feb 1992): 29–33. See also: *The Lancet*, 24 April 1993, p. 1086; 5 June 1993, pp. 1485–6.

Conclusions

1. B. Ehrenreich, quoted in C. Gorman, 'Why Are Men and Women Different?', *Time*, 20 January 1992: 42–51.
2. C. Smart, 'Disruptive Bodies and Unruly Sex', in C. Smart (ed.), *Regulating Womanhood*, London: Routledge, 1992.
3. C. Pateman, 'Equality, Difference, Subordination: The Politics of Motherhood and Women's Citizenship', in G. Bock and S. James (eds), *Beyond Equality and Difference*, London: Routledge, pp. 17–31.
4. D. Haraway, *Simians, Cyborgs and Women*, London: Free Association Books, 1991.
5. A. Wolfe, *Human Difference*, Berkeley, CA: University of California Press, 1993.
6. M. Foucault, *Discipline and Punish: Birth of the Prison*, London: Allen Lane, 1977; *The Birth of the Clinic: An Archaeology of Medical Perception*, London: Tavistock, 1973.
7. M. Strathern, *After Nature: English Kinship in the Late Twentieth Century*, Cambridge: Cambridge University Press, 1992.
8. R. Keat and N. Abercrombie, *Enterprise Culture*, London: Routledge, 1991.
9. S. Helmstetter, *Life Choices: Manage Your Choices, Manage Your Life*, London: Thornsons, 1992.
10. M. Strathern, 'Society in Drag', *Times Higher Education Supplement*, 2 April 1993: 19.
11. M. Hunter and J. Coope, *Time of Her Life: Menopause, Health and Well Being*, London: BBC Books, 1993.
12. K. Backett, 'Taboos and Excesses: Lay Health Moralities in Middle–Class Families', paper given at the British Sociological Association's annual conference, 25–28 March 1991.
13. S. Shuttleworth, 'Patriarchal Science', *Science as Culture*, 2 , (3), no. 12 (1991): 443–57.
14. A. Fausto-Sterling, *Myths of Gender*, revised edn, New York: Basic Books, 1992. See also G. Kaplan and L. Rogers, 'The Definition of Male and Female: Biological Reductionism and the Sanctions of Normality', in S. Gunew (ed.), *Feminist Knowledge, Critique and Construct*, London: Routledge, 1990; L. Birke, '"Life" as We have Known It: Feminism and the Biology of Gender', in M. Benjamin (ed.), *Science and Sensibility: Gender and Scientific Enquiry, 1780–1945*, Oxford: Basil Blackwell, 1991; L. Birke, 'In Pursuit of Difference: Scientific Studies of Women and Men', in G. Kirkup and L.S. Keller (eds), *Inventing Women, Science, Technology and Gender*, Cambridge: Polity Press, 1992.

NOTES

15. S. Harding, *Whose Science? Whose Knowledge? Thinking from Women's Lives*, Milton Keynes: Open University Press, 1991.
16. H. Collins and T. Pinch, *The Golem: What Everyone Should Know About Science*, Cambridge: Cambridge University Press, 1993.
17. S. Shapin, 'Discipline and Bounding: The History and Sociology of Science As Seen Through the Externalism–Internalism Debate', *History of Science* 30 (1992): 333–69.
18. S. LeVay, *The Sexual Brain*, Cambridge, MA: MIT Press, 1992. In July 1993, a team of American scientists claimed to have found good evidence that a 'gay gene' exists. The geneticists did not say they had found the gene, but they think they know where it is – in a region of the X chromosome that boys inherit from their mothers. Analysing the DNA of forty pairs of gay brothers, Dean Hamer and his colleagues at the National Cancer Institute in Bethesda, Maryland, found that most (thirty-three) of the pairs shared the DNA region on the tip of the long arm of the X chromosome (*Science* 261: 321–27). This region clearly cannot be the sole 'cause' of male homosexuality, because seven pairs of gay brothers did not both have that stretch of DNA. Moreover, the statistical link is significant only if certain questionable assumptions are made about how common homosexuality is in the population. Several times in the recent history of human gene research, statistical links as apparently strong as this one have turned out to be artifacts of poor experimental design or of coincidence. Putative genes for alcoholism and schizophrenia have been announced, only to 'disappear' as more data come in. As the American geneticist Mary-Claire King of the University of California at Berkeley wrote in the journal *Nature:* 'The first point to stress is that this result is preliminary. The evidence is based on a small, highly selected group of homosexual men. The result is purely statistical. The gene is hypothetical and has not been cloned, and the linkage has been observed in only one series of families. Were virtually any other trait involved, the paper would have received little public notice until the results have been independently confirmed. But the trait is homosexuality' (*Nature* 364: 288–89). Yet the flurry of newspaper headlines has conveyed a very different message. Many people now wrongly suppose that scientists have 'proven' that people are born gay or straight.
19. D. Swaab, Lecture: 'The Human Hypothalamus in Relation to Gender and Sexual Orientation', 19 November 1992, at AFRC Institute of Animal Physiology and Genetics Research, Cambridge Research Station, Babraham.
20. R. Hubbard, *The Politics of Women's Biology*, New Brunswick: Rutgers University Press, 1990.
21. S. Lipsitz Bem, *The Lenses of Gender: Transforming the Debate on Sexual Inequality*, New Haven, CT: Yale University Press, 1993.
22. S. Oyama, *The Ontogeny of Information: Developmental Systems and Evolution*, Cambridge: Cambridge University Press, 1985.

INDEX